W9-CFB-627

Righteous Indignation

Excuse Me
While I Save the World!

ANDREW BREITBART

GRAND CENTRAL
PUBLISHING

LARGE PRINT

Copyright © 2011 by Andrew Breitbart
All rights reserved. Except as permitted under the U.S. Copyright Act of 1976, no part of this publication may be reproduced, distributed, or transmitted in any form or by any means, or stored in a database or retrieval system, without the prior written permission of the publisher.

Grand Central Publishing

Hachette Book Group
237 Park Avenue
New York, NY 10017

www.HachetteBookGroup.com

Printed in the United States of America

First Edition: April 2011

10 9 8 7 6 5 4 3 2 1

Grand Central Publishing is a division of Hachette Book Group, Inc. The Grand Central Publishing name and logo is a trademark of Hachette Book Group, Inc.

The publisher is not responsible for websites (or their content) that are not owned by the publisher.

Library of Congress Cataloging-in-Publication Data
Breitbart, Andrew.
Righteous indignation : excuse me while I save the world / Andrew Breitbart. — 1st ed.
p. cm.
Includes index.
ISBN 978-0-446-57282-8 (regular edition) — ISBN 978-1-455-50008-6 (large print edition)
1. Journalism — Political aspects — United States. 2. Press and politics — United States. 3. Journalism — Objectivity — United States. 4. United States — Politics and government — 2001–2009. 5. Breitbart, Andrew. I. Title.
PN4888.P6B685 2011
302.230973 — dc22
2010041018

To my dad, Gerald Breitbart, and Clarence Thomas—both decent men who inspired me to act

Contents

Righteous Indignation

CHAPTER I

From Little ACORNs Grow...

In June 2009, I didn't know much about the Association of Community Organizations for Reform Now (ACORN). My attitude toward it was a generic conservative's attitude: I knew that the lack of interest the mainstream media were showing in ACORN—especially with all the accusations leveled against it regarding its illegal voter fraud and ties with the Democratic Party—meant that there had to be something really, truly horrific about it. Whenever there's smoke and the leftist media aren't calling 911, that means there's a huge fire raging out of control somewhere.

But beyond that, I had read only what everyone else had read every election cycle. I had read that ACORN acted as a kind of street army on behalf of Progressive interests, working to get Democrats registered for voting, working to get people on public assistance in the name of "social justice"—and I had read that because of its goals, ACORN was granted absolute protection under the cover of law and the media's willful blindness. I knew that Barack Obama had put ACORN in charge of large swaths of the Census. My e-mail tip box was always filled with questions from readers asking, "What are we going to do about ACORN's Census involvement?"

In 2010, the White House announced that for the 2010 Census, ACORN would recruit 1.4 million workers to go door-to-door counting every person in the country. This in spite of the fact that ACORN had been linked with severe voter fraud in states ranging from Washington to Pennsylvania.[1]

So people were worried. But ACORN was not my number one target by any stretch of the imagination.

Then a young man named James O'Keefe walked into my office.

He showed me a set of videos.

My jaw dropped.

After I watched the videos, there was silence. Then he turned to me and said, "We're going to take down ACORN."

"No," I replied. "We're going to take down the media."

* * *

The September 10, 2009, launch of BigGovernment.com did something President Obama couldn't: it created the first and only bipartisan vote of consequence of his presidency—the congressional defunding of ACORN, a "social and economic justice" advocacy organization key to the electoral infrastructure of the Progressive wing of the Democratic Party and a menacing and destructive "community organizing" group central to Barack Obama's post–Harvard Law years. Within a week of an unorthodox, strategically crafted, staggered release of a series of five videos depicting ACORN workers aiding and abetting a fake pimp and prostitute trying to set up an elaborate sex slave operation, Congress voted unanimously to defund ACORN.

That momentous week changed my life forever. And I believe it helped instigate a winnable New Media war against the Progressive movement and its standard-bearer, President Obama, as well as the vast left-wing media apparatus that rigs the national narrative in the pursuit of partisan politics.

The incredibly courageous work of James O'Keefe ("The Pimp"), then a twenty-five-year-old investigative journalist-cum-Borat of the right, and Hannah Giles, not yet twenty-one at the point of launching the caper, acted as a catalyst for a demoralized conservative movement.

The Hope and Change had begun to wear off in the latter part of the summer of '09, and the Tea Party movement had already begun. But the conservative movement lacked a clear victory to rally the troops around. The ACORN videos became the rallying point of a resurgent conservatism and served as a wake-up call to millions of patriotic Americans that individuals can make a huge difference, especially now with an empowered, media-savvy, Internet army.

That's right, an army.

Make no mistake: America is in a media war. It is an extension of the Cold War that never ended but shifted to an electronic front. The war between freedom and statism ended geographically when the Berlin Wall fell. But the existential battle never ceased.

When the Soviet Union disintegrated, the battle simply took a different form. Instead of missiles the new weapon was language and education, and the international left had successfully constructed a global infrastructure to get its message out.

Schools. Newspapers. Network news. Art. Music. Film. Television.

For decades the left understood the importance of education, art, and messaging.

Oprah Winfrey gets it. David Geffen gets it. Bono gets it. President Barack Obama gets it. Even Corey Feldman gets it.

But the right doesn't. For decades the right felt the Pentagon and the political class and simple common sense could win the day. They were wrong.

The left does not win its battles in debate. It doesn't have to. In the twenty-first century, media is everything. The left wins because it controls the narrative. The narrative is controlled by the media. The left *is* the media. Narrative is everything.

I call it the Democrat-Media Complex—and I am at war to gain back control of the American narrative.

I have allies, veterans who have helped pave the way. Rush Limbaugh and the phenomenon of conservative talk radio are only twenty years old. So desperate was the right for an outlet to express itself that tens of millions now get their information from what was the formerly moribund AM dial.

Please understand that Rush Limbaugh is reviled less for what he says than because he shot the first shot of the New Media war over twenty years ago when he turned AM into the meeting place for America's massive conservative underground. Because of Rush there are countless imitators influencing large amounts of people across America in a billion-dollar talk-radio industry that didn't exist a generation ago.

Matt Drudge and the Drudge Report were met

with relentless attacks from the mainstream media class and the political left during the Clinton years—not because Matt was an aggregator of news stories or a conservative muckraker, but because he created a new front in the long-standing culture war—the Internet. History will look upon Matt Drudge as the Internet's true media visionary. Millions of so-called bloggers write, report, upload their stories online, and influence the national and international political landscape because of the advent of the very liberating and democratic World Wide Web.

And Fox News and its visionary creator Roger Ailes are relentlessly attacked by the same forces— not because Fox News reports the other side of the story, but because it showed that the other side of the story reflects the point of view of more people than CNN.

The constellation of AM talk radio, the Internet (Drudge Report, plus countless bloggers), and Fox News represent the successful, better-late-than-never counterattack against the left's unchallenged control of the culture of a center-right nation. And this counterattack needs field generals, platoon leaders, and foot soldiers ready to storm every hill on the battlefield. To not yield an inch of ground to the ruthless, relentless, shameless enemy we face.

I volunteered to fight in this war. I have risen

through the ranks and now find myself on the front lines with an army of New Media warriors following me into the fray. It is no longer a choice to fight; I am *compelled* to fight. The election of Barack Obama, facilitated by the Democrat-Media Complex that was aligned to usher him into his "rightful and deserved" place in the Oval Office, was the tipping point for my full and unyielding commitment to this war. Why? Because I saw early on that his was literally a made-for-television candidacy.

I knew the fix was in when Oprah Winfrey featured Obama twice on her mega-influential daytime show. One appearance on *Oprah* is enough to make a person a household name. This former state senator and "community organizer" was being given the star treatment as a junior senator from Illinois. For a Democratic Party plagued with sad clown Al Gore in the 2000 election cycle and the ghoulish John Kerry in 2004, charm, youth, and charisma were the obvious components that the next Democratic presidential candidate needed to have.

On the most superficial media level, Barack Obama was a godsend.

Plus he was black. For better, America needed to elect a black president. And the party that elected him or her would forever be granted that historical credit. But also, any criticism of Obama, with his thin résumé and shadowy past, could be framed by a like-minded media class as racism, cowing dissent.

A lifetime of work putting together a media and cultural system to affirm liberal narratives granted Obama a megacatapult to launch him in a way that no Republican or conservative could ever experience.

With the press, the unions, academia, and Hollywood behind Barack Obama, and the American people wanting to get the race monkey off their backs, the Obama presidency was a fait accompli— even if no one really knew anything about him.

My assessment didn't make me popular where I live and raise my young family. Angelenos, especially of the West Los Angeles variety, especially those who work in the entertainment industry, don't take too kindly to dissent—if you are a conservative, that is.

But I was right.

Sure, then-Senator Obama was good-looking— and sleek!—and possessed an undeniable gift for effortless, meaningless gab. But all I could think about was how uninteresting he sounded. With all his power and that massive artificial smile, I couldn't envision wanting to have a beer with him. This was a power-hungry man who rose through the political ranks in corrupt Chicago and through the corrupt ranks of modern academia.

Without having held a real job, without a personal narrative of fulfilling the American Dream in the private sector—without having really *done* anything (achieving greatness only within the confines of political power doesn't cut it)—this man was selling the government, not the individual, as the be-all and end-all. This man was preprogrammed, and I knew what he was selling.

I knew I had to stop him. And the Internet was my battlefield of choice.

I live on the battlefield.

So, here I am. On a United Airlines Boeing 757, 35,000 feet above sea level sans Internet connection, U.S. airspace—my name is Andrew, and I am an Internet addict.

At this point in my 24/7 digital-Wi-Fi life—and, for better or worse, that's what it has been since 1995—I must force myself to the mountains, to the jungle, to the middle of the sea, or to an airline that has yet to install in-flight wireless Internet in order to contemplate life and communicate in a nondigital mode.

And I must do so because I *have* to write this book. I feel it is a moral imperative and a patriotic duty.

It isn't easy. With the thought that I must go off the grid for hours and days on end, my sleep pattern is affected. The waking hours are worse. Old school: there's no other way to write a book. I've watched enough *Oprah* to recognize I must confess something big, embrace my inner victim to get prime network airtime. So bear with me. It all ties in.

I can only write books when truly compelled. The last time I wrote a book (cowrote, actually— *Hollywood, Interrupted*, with Mark Ebner), I had something that needed to be written. This book marks the first time since 2004 that I've felt compelled to communicate a set of ideas that couldn't be related on Twitter or Facebook, on a blog, in a chat room, with AOL Instant Messenger, via Skype, or on Blog Talk Radio.

It's almost unbearable. The Internet jones I've acquired feels like what I hear heroin or cigarette addiction is like. If I wanted it cured, I don't think I would or could. It's what I do. It's now who I am. The flights between Los Angeles and New York and Washington, DC, are especially excruciating. The temporary withdrawals are something fierce. Acute boredom, something the Internet long ago cured, comes back in multiple dimensions. Episodic television, something I grew up on, now angers me. Why? Because I can't control it. I want to go to the menu and delete the laugh track. The plots are plodding. It's all so 1985. Reality TV comes closer to what I want. But I need to *be* Mark Burnett and Simon Cowell, not to live vicariously through them and the worlds they are creating. The best I can hope for in this Brave New Wired World is that in the future the Andrew Breitbart Center for Internet Addiction can help future generations of digital-heads.

For now, I embrace the sickness because it reaps great rewards. In the few dimensions in which I reside, my life could not be better. The war for the soul of a nation, and perhaps the world, is being fought in the New Media. And I am right in the middle of it. My "Big" Internet sites hit the ground running and are breaking the types of stories that major newspapers and networks broke in the past.

As long as I'm in confession mode, I'll admit I am also addicted to breaking news stories—big, medium, and small. I don't care whether you call me a journalist, a reporter, a muckraker, or a rabble-rouser, just give me the goods. Let's get the story out there.

There is no greater high than watching cable news or listening to talk radio and seeing stories that five minutes before were in Microsoft Word format now playing themselves out, sometimes with major consequence, on the world stage.

My dual afflictions—addiction to the Internet and addiction to breaking stories—together constitute a New Media addiction. And as a New Media addict I am both junkie and supplier.

Big Hollywood contributor Patrick Courrielche, a brave Hollywood-based artist and media entrepreneur whose name and heroics will play out later in the book, broke the White House/National Endowment for the Arts scandal that led to a top NEA employee's resignation. After things started to settle down, Patrick and I shared words about the fact that circumventing Old Media by using New Media, forcing them to cover the story and to shape, control, and even change narratives, was a once-in-a-lifetime experience.

I felt like a New Media Sherpa. I took Patrick to the plateau and he saw what could be done. He continues to search for the next Big story. It will come. I know it. Patrick is but one in a growing stable of Big contributors to my Big group blog sites—sites that you'll find out about later in this book—that are tapping into a renaissance of investigative journalism and participatory democracy.

The adrenaline that fuels my psyche is almost always in an optimal state. The excitement of the battle, the victories—they're piling up. The enemy is not used to being attacked at foundational levels. With every online victory, new recruits are joining the army. Things are too good right now to worry about something so trite as whether I'm frying my cerebral cortex.

The Internet has changed and is changing everything—including the way my brain works. Am I the only one? For this radical rewiring of everything there are pros and cons. Many industries are failing—newspapers, most obviously. But Knight Ridder and McClatchy's loss is James O'Keefe's, Hannah Giles's, Matt Drudge's, Jim Robinson's (Free Republic), Lucianne Goldberg's, Arianna Huffington's, and Andrew Breitbart's gain.

If the newspapers weren't so close to the situation, and the implosion of the Old Media didn't involve the livelihoods of those covering the revolution, reporters and journalists would recognize this moment as the beginning of a massive global information awakening.

These are big times. The expansion of freedom in the digital world will lead to the expansion of freedom in the real world.

The people of the United States, with its First Amendment, are leading the way in combining free speech and technology. Just as Western rock and roll helped bring down the Eastern Bloc in the latter half of the twentieth century, the Internet is going to provide a similar impetus to the people of the world to grasp the possibilities of freedom.

In the entire history of the world, these are the most exciting times to live in.

If the political left weren't so joyless, humorless, intrusive, taxing, overtaxing, anarchistic, controlling, rudderless, chaos-prone, pedantic, unrealistic, hypocritical, clueless, politically correct, angry, cruel, sanctimonious, retributive, redistributive, intolerant—and if the political left weren't hell-bent on expansion of said unpleasantness into all aspects of my family's life—the truth is, I would not be in your life.

If the Democratic Party were run by Joe Lieberman and Evan Bayh, if it had the slightest vestige of JFK and Henry "Scoop" Jackson, I wouldn't be on the political map.

If the American media were run by biased but not evil Tim Russerts and David Brinkleys, I wouldn't have joined the fight.

Except for about 3,213 people (friends, family, and former acquaintances), you would not know who I am.

You would not be reading this book—because I would not have written it.

If the college campus weren't filled with tenured professors like 9/11 apologist Ward Churchill and bullshit departments like Queer Studies, and if the academic framework weren't being planned out by domestic terrorists like Bill Ayers, I wouldn't be expanding my Internet media empire to include Big Education.

If art wasn't almost exclusively defined by degradation of cultural norms—unless when promoting an all-knowing "HOPE"-ful leftist leader, I wouldn't be spraying my Jackson Pollock political/cultural musings on the American New Media cultural canvas.

If America's pop-cultural ambassadors like Alec Baldwin and Janeane Garofalo didn't come back from their foreign trips to tell us how much they hate us, if my pay cable didn't highlight a comedy show every week that called me a racist for embracing constitutional principles and limited government, I wouldn't be at Tea Parties screaming my love for this great, charitable, and benevolent country.

The left made me do it! I swear!

I am a reluctant cultural warrior.

CHAPTER 2

Lost in the Complex

Like millions of others of my (graying) generation, I spent my adolescence as a pop-culture-infused, wannabe hipster and mindless consumer. I was the ultimate Generation X slacker, not particularly political, and, in retrospect, a default liberal. I thought that going to four movies a week, knowing the network television grid, and spending hours at Tower Records were my American birthright. As a middle-class kid growing up in upper-middle-class Brentwood, my parents went overboard to provide me the highest standard of living. And I took advantage of their overwhelming generosity.

Brentwood is a high-end subsection of Los Angeles. While Brentwood holds a mythic place in the consciousness of the American people as *the* upscale suburb filled with celebrities and the wealthy, the Brentwood I grew up in was more like the neighborhood from *E.T.* or *The Brady Bunch*. Even though it was very much a keep-up-with-the-Joneses enclave, my parents seemed oblivious to all that. When the first sushi restaurant popped up in our neighborhood in the early 1980s, we had meat loaf that night.

I knew that Gerry and Arlene Breitbart, my parents, were Republicans only because when they would come back from Mount St. Mary's College, their local polling place, I would pry the information from them. I remember finding out that they voted for Ford in 1976, Bush in the 1980 Republican primaries against Reagan, and Reagan both times in the 1980 and 1984 national elections.

But at the same time, they never talked about their politics. They came from the Silent Generation. My mother existed as a perfect exemplar of that generation, as though she were destined to be a grandmother from birth. She spoke in aphorisms like "Children should be seen and not heard" and "Don't talk politics or religion at the dinner table." Whenever any form of contention arose at our dinner table, she'd awkwardly interject a non sequitur: "Your aunt Ethel makes the most perfect rhubarb pie!" I swear. Rhubarb pie.

My parents didn't speak their politics; they acted on them. Their attitudes toward the people around them living the Hollywood liberal lifestyle were grounded in a reality and a normalcy and a decency. My father ran a restaurant in Santa Monica; my mom worked at a bank. I would often ask my father, "Which famous people come into the restaurant?" For some odd, infuriating reason, he would always say, "All of my customers are the same. I don't care about those things." And he meant it. I would later force my mother to tell me that the Reagans and Broderick Crawford and Shirley Jones and the Cassidy family, among many, many others, were regulars at the English-style steakhouse called the Fox and Hounds. Not only did my father *not* put these people on a pedestal, but fifteen hours a day, seven days a week, he treated all his customers and employees as individuals and as human beings.

I've always felt that people reveal themselves in their vacation choices, a belief probably stemming from my childhood. While many of my friends' parents were gallivanting off to Europe and leaving their kids at home—for some reason, my parents considered this a form of child abuse—my parents opted to buy a thirty-three-foot motor home, the Executive, and took my sister and me on a formative cross-country trip that I daydream about even now. It was my first real taste of the America that I defend to this day. My dad seemed like another human being on the road, and he engaged with every possible stranger he could—he even changed his Chicago Jewish accent and developed a twang as we entered the Wild West. It was so clear how much he liked people. When people wonder why I will talk to a lamppost, I point to my dad.

My parents granted me a brilliant middle-class life, one that didn't overwhelm and lavish spoils on me to the point of absurdity. The house was not filled with objects or celebrities that would cause my friends to envy me, wish they could live at my house, or hang out with our social circle. My parents were also about fifteen years older than some of my friends' parents, so while my mother was watching Lawrence Welk on television on Saturday nights, one of my friends' dads rented a limousine so he could hit the Rod Stewart and Bryan Ferry concerts in the same night. While my parents' house had a pool and four bedrooms and a scenic canyon view of West Los Angeles, it couldn't compete with the beachfront Malibu property that two of my friends at school occupied. And I'm ashamed to admit: those families existed in an ether that became growingly intoxicating to me.

Along with my friends' parents' elite addresses came original art, celebrity friends, and a very specific brand of liberal politics. Bobby Kennedy, to this crowd, did not just represent a political philosophy, but an aesthetic that started to lure me away from my parents' simple, grounded nature. That, and those pesky palpitations in my loins. Between the lure of a greater material life and my emerging sexual teen persona, my parents' chaste, safe haven became less and less appealing, other than as a place to catch some Zzzzs and get three free square meals. And in a gesture of trust, my parents granted me the independence to start becoming my own person. (I still cry myself to sleep wishing that they had fought harder to keep me in that protective cocoon!)

My lifestyle began to change as I hit puberty and high school. I recall those years as spent ignoring school as best as possible while spending weekends at the best beaches and private houses, behind gates and tall bushes. I took tennis lessons with Steve Morris, the top tennis pro in Malibu, the same guy who taught Farrah Fawcett, Bruce Jenner, Arnold Schwarzenegger, and the entire tennis-playing Van Patten family (Joyce, Dick, Vince, Nels, and Jimmy). After one of those lessons, I vividly recall Schwarzenegger, before his ascent into megastardom, literally terrorizing me and my best friend, Larry Solov, by hitting ball after ball as hard as he could at us, to the point where we wailed in the corner and he cackled aloud. Yes, the Governator is one sadistic bastard. And, yes, I voted for him.

Another time, Farrah Fawcett asked me where Steve was. I led her on a fifteen-minute wild-goose chase looking for him just so I could hang out with her for a bit. I've never felt so cool, before or since.

But every time I came home from my tennis lessons or my elite private school or these exclusive beach houses, I would come home to the cold, stark reality that I was living someone else's lifestyle, not the one that my parents could afford or would have chosen for me. The closest my family got to the prestige of that world was that we once rented out our motor home to John Ritter from *Three's Company*. I bragged about it in school for weeks.

Then, the ultimate indignity. When I was sixteen years old, in order to keep up with my friends, I needed to supplement what my parents were willing to give me as an allowance. I needed to get a job.

Delivering pizza for Maria's was probably the greatest job I have ever had. During my last two years in high school, even during baseball and football season, after practice, I would make a small nightly fortune driving my dark gray Honda Prelude to some of the best real estate in America, to some of the most famous (and occasionally generous) people in the world. Listening to The Smiths while delivering a spinach calzone to Judge Reinhold in Westwood was bliss. I soon discovered that having sixty or eighty tax-free dollars in my pocket after each shift only enhanced a growing sense of freedom, of independence. I thought I was becoming an adult. It was around this time that I met Mike.

You remember meeting these people as an adolescent. The ones who immediately intrigue you, who seem to intimate vast, unknown continents of knowledge and experience. Mike was one—a mysterious coworker two years my senior who went to school across town. Because we shared the same teenage passion for a very specific type of angst-driven British alt-rock—the The, New Order, The Jam, Paul Weller, The Style Council, Aztec Camera, Fun Boy Three, The Specials, The Cure, Depeche Mode—we became instant friends. He knew more about this brooding genre than even I did. But his greatest influence on me was his hyperinformed and deeply philosophical roots in left-wing politics.

Mike, like me, was working as a disinterested student, educating himself off curricula. Where I was self-taught by way of news media and pop culture, Mike was informed by the highbrow literary and philosophical tracts of obscure political philosophers. His vocal politics challenged the order that I had long taken for granted. After all, I had no problem with my life. In fact, I liked it a lot. But after years of going to concerts with Mike, and going to local coffee shops and visiting alternative bookstores with him, Mike, like a self-appointed mentor, adopted me as a project. And since I was an avowed C+ student and secretly felt I deserved Ds, Mike's intellectualism was the epitome of sexy to me. I not only started to read the works of Alan Watts and the ethereal musings of Richard Bach, I also delved into the *Utne Reader* and *LA Weekly*—both bastions of leftist thinking.

Needless to say, Mike was the exact opposite of my father. He was fascinating. He took the SATs for his friends at his high school. He even wrote papers for them. He got them into the best colleges. And where my father valued hard work above everything, Mike valued intellect above everything. My father had an innate moral compass; Mike had none. But his amoral righteousness was born of a contempt for the existing political and economic paradigms. Except for a self-made ethos of friendship, he reveled in being valueless.

Mike gave me a CliffsNotes version of the leftist point of view, a romanticized, James Dean–ish, moral-relativist, everything-is-pointless crash course on how thinking people should, in fact, think. I imbibed it without question. So when it came time for college, it was as if the professors in my freshman classes were speaking the exact same language he was. Through some form of osmosis, I considered myself a liberal. As a result, there would be no culture shock when I entered Tulane.

While skipping college was never a possibility, my decision-making process for choosing the right one was the exact opposite of all of my peers'. To quote the Red Hot Chili Peppers, I wanted to rock out with my cock out. After all, Mike had taught me that nothing mattered anyway. Might as well have fun in the meantime.

I put more effort into choosing the correct party school than I did into studying during my entire high-school career. And because I had older friends who went to state schools where beer bongs and the frat boy experience were as generic as it appears in the movies, I believed that I had to go to a higher place. I had to up the ante.

New Orleans.

There happens to be a school there called Tulane. When somebody said to me, "Oh, it's a respectable school"—bingo!

In one of the more popular college guidebooks, I recall Tulane described in terms of how many bars there were in the surrounding region. It said that you could go to a different bar every night during your time at Tulane, and never repeat. That book was not lying. The first two weeks of Tulane reminded me of basic training scenes in films where the recruit doesn't seem like he is going to make it.

I thought I could drink when I came to Tulane. I had some hard-and-fast rules to prevent becoming an alcoholic, such as: don't drink during sunlight hours. By the end of my time at Tulane, I was going to bed so early in the morning and waking up so late in the afternoon that this rule was almost impossible to break. Thank God I wasn't developing a drinking problem.

Now, where I think I made a wrong turn was when I was taken under the wing of a very particular clique in my new fraternity, Delta Tau Delta. These guys were from the northeast tristate area: Connecticut, New York, and New Jersey. And one from California — me. They wrongly assumed from the film portrayal of high-school life in the Hollywood of the 1980s (think *Less Than Zero*) that I was a hard-living, cocaine-fueled man of a thousand lovers.

Perhaps I led them on.

Because in no time, I was.

Any standards I had retained to this point, as well as that little thing I called my virginity, became objects in the rearview mirror very quickly. Not only were my new friends decadent, funny, and sick bastards, there was nothing resembling an adult authority figure in that godforsaken town. Moderation is just not in that city's DNA.

On a Tuesday night, for instance, one could find himself at a drinking establishment by the name of F & M on Tchoupitoulas Street, dancing atop a pool table with twenty other denizens of New Orleans—black, white, and Creole; young, middle-aged, and old. Stumbling out of the bar, ready to head on to the next one, a police officer in uniform would stop anyone leaving with a bottle of beer—not to admonish the reveler but rather to helpfully remind him that he must transfer his beer into a plastic "Geaux cup." I shamefully recall getting behind the wheel of my car with such a Geaux cup, lifting up the beer and giving an officer a cheer as I drove away, off to the Rendon Inn. Even the law enforcement in New Orleans reinforced the 24/7 debauchery.

Truth be told, I was at first horrified by the behavior around me. I do recall at one point musing about my choice of college, "This might've been a significant mistake." But because I had my first serious girlfriend on campus, leaving was not an option.

So I distinctly chose to do as the Romans did.

With the passing of every drunken and debauched week, I could feel the acute sense of right and wrong that had been bestowed upon me by my parents fading further away. I started to see things in shades of gray. And the courses that I was supposedly taking, mostly in the Humanities department, seemed to jibe perfectly with this new outlook.

One day, I went to my campus mailbox and found a letter that informed me that I was months late in declaring my major. I had been avoiding the decision because not one professor or one class had sufficiently moved me like the young prep school stallions in *Dead Poets Society* had been. I would have been happy with Rodney Dangerfield from *Back to School*.

But no such luck. So as I walked out of the student union with that letter in hand, I marched up to an attractive group of blonde coeds with whom I was socially familiar. Part to make them laugh and part to finally make up my mind, I told them that by the end of our conversation, they would decide my major for me. After less than five minutes of discussing my academic interests or lack thereof, we decided upon American Studies. What a stud, huh?

The virtue of the ambiguous American Studies degree for a creative loafer like me was that it was both an interdisciplinary and an interdepartmental major. I recognized that I could play the different department heads off of each other. To my English professors, I could say, "English is not my strong suit." I also found out that this same tactic worked in the History and Philosophy departments as well.

American Studies etched my wayward trajectory in stone—it ensured I would accomplish nothing in the next few years. The visits back to my Los Angeles reality for Christmas and summer breaks became intrusions into my consciousness. I was becoming a dissolute Southern literary figure without the depth, character development, or literary output.

At this point, I was living in two worlds: my LA world and my New Orleans world. My LA friends, my New Orleans friends. My daytime, my nighttime. When I wasn't busy loving my new life, I was horrified and self-loathing. There were only highs and lows. There were no mediums.

Around the beginning of my sophomore year, I made yet another excellent lifestyle choice and moved across the way from one of the country's most notorious college bookies. So while my roommates were betting $50 and $100 per game on college football games on Saturday and pro games on Sunday (and of course, *Monday Night Football*), I opted to live vicariously through their wins and losses...for a while. And by "a while" I mean about a month.

I started to dabble in $20 bets. There was no

pizza delivery route in New Orleans. So my money, at this point, was the $300 monthly stipend my parents were giving me. But as the cliché goes, that $20 wasn't enough action, and so I started getting into the $50 and $100 bets. I started gambling on backgammon, too (I'm not a bad player). This became another means of blowing money that I wasn't earning. But thank God for my accelerating drinking problem—it cut down on the time I had to gamble.

My sleep patterns became so irregular that I started to resemble the characters in Anne Rice's New Orleans–based works. The funny thing about sleeping—and this holds true to this day—is that as I would drift into sleep, that's when the harrowing reminders of what my life had become would visit me. I knew that, at some point, I would have to do an about-face, to change everything. But I didn't know how, and to be honest, the cons of this lifestyle had yet to outweigh the pros.

My favorite pastime during this four-year phase was to lure my high-school friends down to New Orleans for a weekend, preferably Mardi Gras or Halloween. During those two- to three-day forays, I would afford them the trip of a lifetime, showing them things that they couldn't imagine, bewildering them with the euphoria of the 24/7 surreal New Orleans lifestyle. During these benders, I would try to convince myself I was having fun, too. But when I would take them to the airport to send them off, where they would thank me for the most spectacularly wild weekend of their lives, as they got on the plane, I'd feel the deepest despair. And under my breath, I'd say, "Take me with you."

Did I mention that I liked a lot of the people that I was at school with? Some were funny. A couple of the ladies even let me be inside of them. So don't get me wrong. My time was not completely misused. It just wasn't productive in any way, shape, or form. And at heart, I knew it.

At one critical point in my sophomore year, I went to the head of my department to explain that I was in over my head, and to make matters worse, I had just been dumped by my girlfriend. And she, one of the only ostensible adults in my life in New Orleans, suggested that I take a semester off and go drop acid in New York. She really said that.

Good idea, Teach! So I went.

You don't need to hear about it—you can guess. I came back from a semester in New York, where I spent $23,500 that I had inherited from a great-aunt I didn't really know...on nothing. Not to wax too philosophical, but beers in New York are twice as expensive as they are in New Orleans.

So with that valuable life lesson, I went back to New Orleans, $23,500 poorer, entering what would have been my junior year with the number of credits an incoming sophomore would have.

Now, don't ask me how I did what came next. Even I don't know. But somehow, I made a commitment to myself to graduate with my class. I had no great epiphany. I did not have a transformation that one could see in a montage in a movie where I started to hit the books frantically. I just willed myself to do it. I think it was some atavistic self-preservation.

I needed to reach the finish line. I needed to get out of that place.

I also vowed to rid myself of this nasty little gambling habit—and attendant debt—I'd developed. The low point: taking my friend Scott into my walk-in closet, saying he could have whatever he wanted for fifty dollars. He took my leather jacket. So one day, I called my mother and divulged my bind. In an exceptionally calm manner, she gave me the stern maternal talking-to that I desperately needed. She then sent me a check to cover my debt. I paid it. And that was the last of my dealings with my bookie. Moms can do that to you.

By now, I knew that graduating was less about getting the degree than it was getting my release papers from New Orleans. Pushing myself through my credit quandary would take more than will—it would take finesse. I hadn't fulfilled my math requirement, mostly because it was the only course that had a mandatory attendance requirement. I had dropped it my first semester, my second semester, and my third semester. At the time, I remember thinking, *By the time I'm a senior, I'll have my act together, and I'll pay attention. I know I'll be a better student by my senior year.*

Yeah, right.

So the last semester, I had to take math. If my Humanities professors thought I was giving them short shrift, this poor Chinese grad student whose job it was to instill in me the basics of precalculus got no shrift. He went shriftless. Going into the final, my last week of class during senior year, I knew less than the day the class started. My test-taking strategy for this, my last test of my woeful college career, was figuring *I'm twenty-two years old. I've got to know more about this subject than the average fifteen-year-old high-school student.*

Wrong!

The test had twenty questions. As is customary, they required correct answers. And to make matters worse, apparently they wanted me to show my work. After a look through the twenty questions, I noticed that the first was the easiest, and each question was more difficult than the previous one, so that the last was the hardest. After I stared at question one for about fifteen minutes, hoping that I would be inspired, waiting for the math muse, I realized that today was not going to be my day.

I started to see my life passing before my eyes. I started to consider that maybe years of skating by, recklessly expecting everything to work out, had been exactly the wrong approach to derivatives. It was a big moment for someone raised on—and among—the trusty happy endings of Hollywood. Apparently, I realized, sometimes it *doesn't* work out. Sometimes you have to *make* it work out. Which means: maybe values *do* matter. I took a deep breath, stood up, walked toward the teacher, as the rest of the class scribbled away—and asked that he join me outside the classroom.

I said, "Sir, I'm going to be frank with you here. I need to graduate. I have family and friends coming in from out of town tomorrow. We have reservations at Commander's Palace. Failing this class is not going to serve either of our needs. Now, the way I look at it, I'm not going into a career in science or math. I think we can agree upon that. I'm not asking for your answer right now. I just wanted to put this into your head. Perhaps you could see my flawed humanity and allow for me to move on with my life."

Even though English was not his first language, he got the message. I called the next day and he gave me a passing grade in the class (a C–, I believe). In the end, I graduated with just above a 2.0.

The next day, my parents and family friends, the Solovs, came to celebrate my graduation from Sodom and Gomorrah. At star chef Susan Spicer's Bayona restaurant (delicious!), my academic career was toasted.

Joanne Solov, my friend Larry's mother, asked me, "So what are you going to do now that you've graduated?"

With utter sincerity, I told the table, "Well, over the next year, I'm going to start trying to wake up before noon."

The next day was my flight back to Los Angeles, a Delta Airlines nonstop. And back then, they used to give a complimentary USA *Today*. I remember this because the above-the-fold headline was "Graduates Entering Worst Economy In Decade."

Terrific!

Thankfully, with this American Studies degree, I knew I would have a competitive edge.

As the plane took off, I envisioned myself, like the protagonist in a big-budget Simpson/Bruckheimer film, walking away from an exploding cityscape and not looking backward, not even for a second.

From the earliest age, I had always had a profound sense of right and wrong. During college, however, I saw the world through the prism of moral relativism and grays, and my own personal standards simply went away somewhere. Okay, fair enough. I was young. But now, I needed them back. I didn't consider this political, nor did I see this as theological. It just was my internal voice telling me I had to straighten up. Who knows where it came from — my parents, my solid upbringing, I'd guess. Perhaps coming back to Los Angeles, where my family and friends lived, I felt that I needed to return to the Andrew Breitbart that these people expected.

In addition to that, my parents did what they probably should have done as I entered college: they cut me off financially. It's hard to explain to the average person what upper-middle-class entitlement feels like, because when you no longer have it and you recognize how pathetic it is, it becomes a point of embarrassment. My work ethic in high school provided me goodies, the extras of life. Now I needed money to live. So I got a job waiting tables at Hal's in Venice.

When I got my first paycheck, when I got my first day's worth of tips while waiting at Hal's, and I had to apply that to rent, to shoes, to rice, to the basic necessities of life, I was in shock. How on God's green earth did everybody do this?

But buying my first pair of shoes with my own money was an Emersonian epiphany. That was one of the first baby steps toward embracing adulthood and maturity, something that being on the easy parental dole could never provide. I felt like Andrew Carnegie in those shoes.

A second step toward self-actualization was the experience of waiting tables on friends from high school and college who happened in on my lowly afternoon wait shift. Twice, friends asked me with a look of great worry on their faces, "Why are you doing this?" The peer pressure that had defined so much of my high-school years in Brentwood and the mostly wealthy clique that I spent time with at Tulane meant that if I joined the club, I would be a member of the elite. To fall outside of the boundaries of that upper-middle-classness wasn't merely unacceptable; it simply wasn't an option. And here I was, waiting on my former peers hand and foot.

I'd spent many years in Brentwood and at Tulane scoffing at my friends who fretted about their futures. Now here I was, watching those same people in law school, medical school, or working in jobs in buildings that I didn't even know how to enter. Nothing like a dose of complete humiliation to make you realize how completely full of shit you are.

But strangely, it felt good. I knew the only place to go was up.

Instead of being deflated by the realization that my friends had the answers and had figured out how to get respectable jobs right out of college, I was just happy with the expectation that somebody was waiting for me to do a job. *Baby steps,* I told myself. My years in New Orleans began to appear more and more ludicrous to me. I'd thought I was some sort of standard-bearer, stumbling home at daylight every morning. It felt significantly less maverick to be informing my childhood friends what the soup of the day was. I was beginning to understand that my self-worth was in direct proportion to how hard I applied myself to productive pursuits. My values were returning from exile.

Even as I was discovering the fulfillment I could derive from hard work, I was still a default liberal. Around this time, I watched the Clarence Thomas confirmation hearings with the alacrity of a boxing fan at the Ali-Frazier fight. It was a major media event and a political heavyweight match. The way that the media had billed it, the Rocky Balboa was Anita Hill. She was the protagonist. The only people in Clarence Thomas's corner were members of the Republican Party. And to me, they were the scolds, the hypocrites, the town elders in *Footloose,* the people who represented the people who would give over their hard-earned money to Jim and Tammy Bakker in exchange for eternal salvation. My perspective on the political process was an inch deep. But my desire to see Clarence Thomas's blood was immense.

So when the opening bell rang, I was expecting Hill to deliver a relentless barrage of accusations and evidence about a man whose behavior around women was professionally unacceptable. I expected lurid details of intimidation, coercion, and harassment. But Hill and her allies described a workplace and a boss-employee relationship that seemed utterly unremarkable. To listen to the media commentators affirm the outrage of Democratic female harpies, parroting the overwrought cries of Anita as channeled by this driven core of Democratic officials, was infuriating—it was so obviously unjust. (Leading the questioning, by the way: Senators Howard Metzenbaum, Pat Leahy, Joe Biden, and Teddy Kennedy.)

Now I may have been a Democrat. I may have been a liberal. But I was not stupid. Something was very wrong here. The melodrama did not come close to matching the lack of evidence that was being presented. They were accusing Thomas of spotting a pubic hair on a soda can, of asking Hill on a date. There was no "there" there. It was ridiculous.

I was perfectly aware at the time that the Democrats were motivated by the abortion issue. And at the time, I was pro-choice. So when Thomas's inquisitors pierced the sanctity of the "right to privacy" that is the hallmark of left-wing constitutional rights, flaunting that they had discovered through illicit means that Thomas had rented pornography, my mental anguish turned physical. I writhed in agony and actually threw a shoe at the television set.

At the same time, it was impossible for me to not recognize that Clarence Thomas's being black was part of the story. How in hell could white Americans Leahy, Biden, and Metzenbaum, let alone former KKK grand pooh-bah Robert Byrd and Chappaquiddick's very own Ted Kennedy, so arrogantly excoriate this man whose personal narrative from sharecropper's grandson to Supreme Court nominee embodied the American dream? A narrative that would send a clear signal to African-Americans that anything is possible in this country? Why were so many white Democrats in the media and in the political class working in concert to assassinate this man's character and to stop that dream in its tracks?

During this media feeding frenzy my eyes were opened, perhaps for the first time, to the fact that something was awry in American political and media life. What secret bit did Kennedy and Biden know about the NAACP, ABC, NBC, and CBS that they could grill a black man on such weak

charges and know that those politically correct entities would not savage them? If the tables were
turned and Clarence Thomas were a liberal Democrat, the NAACP wouldn't have waited a second.
Somehow, these white male senators of privilege
knew that they could get away with it.

My sympathy for Thomas was utter and complete. I wanted to stop the hearings. I wanted him
to be issued public, formal apologies. I naïvely expected that the press would do the job of forcing
those apologies. I could understand how the mainstream media could accept Anita Hill and Con-
gresswoman Pat Schroeder at their word. But even
if the accusations were true, they amounted to
nothing. Certainly a hell of a lot less than what
Senator Kennedy likely did to his female staff on
any given Washington workday. This was, as Clarence Thomas perfectly stated, an electronic lynch-
ing.

And the media aided and abetted it.

Please note that I did not leave the Clarence
Thomas hearings a Republican. I did not leave the
hearings an originalist. But I did leave the hearings
deeply cynical of media that I had thought were
neutral and a Democratic Party that I'd believed
was guided by principle. This was the beginning of
the end of the self-deception that I was like everyone else around me. It would take a few more years

to get there—to discover that I was a conservative—but this was the exact point where I realized that it was not just that I disagreed with the Democratic Party but, more important, that the media were its dominant partner in crime. The national disgrace that was the Clarence Thomas confirmation hearings, for me, changed everything.

This is not the point in the story where we cue the montage of success.

Based on the available evidence—that the only tangible skill set I had was that I could make people laugh, and that I was in Los Angeles—I took the first available job in Hollywood with the hope that I'd eventually become a comedy writer.

Hollywood is anything but a meritocracy. So I thought I'd try to leverage some old friends to insert myself into the world that was the backdrop of my childhood. Through a friend, I got a runner position at a low-budget movie production company in Santa Monica. Over a period of a year, I put 22,000 miles on the Saab convertible that I'd bought when I graduated college. Its quality was a constant and painful reminder that I hadn't earned the money for it, but in the exceptionally shallow town that is Hollywood, my boss took an immediate liking to me based on his false perception that I was of his status. With the $230 that he was paying me per week, I couldn't afford my own car payments, let alone running around with his Hollywood crowd. But I learned that that was exactly what I had to do in order to get ahead in that business.

For a year I delivered scripts around town, entering every single Hollywood office of note, including Michael Ovitz's, Jeffrey Katzenberg's, and Michael Eisner's. It wasn't long before I saw clearly what made Hollywood run. I realized that the town was about relationships, about ass-kissing, about groupthink, about looking over the shoulder of the person you're having a conversation with to see if there's somebody more important in the room that you should be speaking to. I just as quickly realized that this was not my world. I had spent the last four years of my life in college subordinating myself to a system that ran against my better instincts. I was not going to make that mistake again.

So while the producer was incentivizing me to become production staff—he even gave me control over a project, *Valley Girl 2* (thank God that was never made)—I did everything in my power to stay in my car doing the lowly runner job because I didn't want to get sucked in further.

And in my car was AM radio.

My habit came about accidentally. My devotion to KROQ FM and San Diego's 91X, trailblazing alternative rock stations, began to fade with the invasion of the grunge rock movement. Soundgarden, Pearl Jam, Alice in Chains, Mudhoney, Blind Melon, Screaming Trees were replacing The Cure, New Order, The English Beat, Echo and the Bunnymen. It was like watching your youth get cancelled. And my hatred of grunge was visceral. The forced thrift-shop flannel look belied Los Angeles's temperate weather. Who were these whiny, suicidal freaks? I didn't want to know, I just wanted them off my car radio.

So in an act of absolute and pure desperation, I flipped the dial to AM.

As a social animal, I abhor sitting in a room by myself. I love the exchange of ideas. And in listening to talk radio, there was an artificial sensation that I was part of a conversation. I quickly discovered that I would do anything to listen to talk radio. When I would deliver a script out in Burbank at Disney Studios, I developed a technique where I could put an AM Sports Walkman on my ears in my car while I was listening to the radio, so that when I got out of the car to do my five- to ten-minute delivery, I could remain part of the conversation. I went out of my way to avoid underground parking. I even started jogging because it gave me an excuse to listen more. I listened to so much talk radio I was actually able to run in the 1994 Los Angeles Marathon. Four hours, for those wondering.

My first forays into embracing a specific host were Jim Rome and Howard Stern. Both of them clearly used humor and strong opinion to engage their listeners. But it was during the 1992 election cycle that so much of the conversation on the AM dial was built around politics.

In 1992, I certainly still considered myself a Democrat. Jerry Brown was my candidate in the primaries, and he really hooked me on his criticism of Gov. William Jefferson Clinton of Arkansas. People talk about the vast right-wing conspiracy being the origins of anti-Clinton rhetoric. But Brown's campaign was the prototype. He was talking Whitewater and pointing to the fact that this was a typical Arkansas Democratic machine, a political force, not a political reformer. I had experienced the colorful yet corrupt politics of Louisiana for four years—including the proudly corrupt politics of Gov. Edwin Edwards—so putting the chief executive of Arkansas, a state with a similar MO, in charge seemed to me an unwise choice.

While working at this Roger Corman–esque production company, I was getting quite serious with my now wife, Susie. Not only was I working in Hollywood, I was dating the daughter of Orson Bean, an actor, comedian, and raconteur. Spending time at his house on the Venice canals (which to this day I still call Dennis Kucinich Bumper Sticker Country—where Clinton, Kerry, and Obama aren't left enough), I perused his bookshelves. Not only was I attracted to Susie, I was attracted to Orson's wit and depth of knowledge of *everything*. This guy had appeared on the *Tonight Show* couch seventhmost of any guest. His opinion mattered to me.

One day I asked him why he had Rush Limbaugh's book *The Way Things Ought to Be* on his shelf. I asked him, "Why would you have a book by this guy?"

And Orson said, "Have you ever listened to him?"

I said yes, of course, even though I never had. I was convinced to the core of my being that Rush Limbaugh was a Nazi, anti-black, anti-Jewish, and anti–all things decent. Without berating me for disagreeing with him, Orson simply suggested that I listen to him again.

While I was listening to Jim Rome and Howard Stern, the intensity of the 1992 election cycle warranted that I switch the frequency over to hearing about the horse race.

This is where my rendezvous with destiny begins.

I turned on KFI 640 AM to listen to evil personified from 9 a.m. to noon. Indeed, my goal was to derive pleasure from the degree of evil I found in Rush Limbaugh. I was looking forward to a jovial discussion with Orson to confirm how right I was.

One hour turned into three. One listening session into a week's worth. And next thing I knew, I was starting to doubt my preprogrammed self. I was still a Democrat. I was still a liberal.

But after listening for months while putting thousands of miles on my car, I couldn't believe that I once thought this man was a Nazi or anything close. While I couldn't yet accept the premise that he was speaking my language, I marveled at how he could take a breaking news story and offer an entertaining and clear analysis that was like nothing I had ever seen on television, especially the Sunday morning shows, which had been my previous one-stop shop for my political opinions.

Most important, though, Limbaugh, like the professor I always wanted but never had the privilege to study under, created a vivid mental picture of the architecture of a world that I resided in but couldn't see completely: the Democrat-Media Complex. Embedded in Limbaugh's analysis of politics was always a tandem discussion on the media. Each segment relentlessly pointed to collusion between the media and the Democratic Party. If the Clarence Thomas hearings showed me that something was wrong, the ensuing years of listening to Limbaugh and Dennis Prager—who at the time was also undergoing a political transformation from the Democratic to the Republican Party—explained to me with eerie precision what exactly was wrong. I swallowed hard and conceded to Orson that he was right.

And so it began.

The default labels of liberal and Democrat—labels that were necessary cultural accessories in my Hollywood and Venice worlds—were becoming ill-fitting.

I still had a natural disdain for the religious right, which had been the ultimate 1980s-era bogeyman, so I was looking for some neutral ground while I tried to figure things out. If you met me in 1992, for some odd reason, I would have told you I was a libertarian, and I voted for Ross Perot. The only awkward memory that haunts me more is my roller-disco period.

While Professor Limbaugh provided me an understanding of the architecture of how politics and media relate, Professor Prager provided me articulation of the ethical framework my parents had lived out. I saw that my parents were fundamentally right and that those ecstatically exuberant and audaciously fun New Orleans years came at a great cost. I knew that I was estranged from my parents' belief system and that a permanently libertine lifestyle was no substitute for a clean conscience, work that felt satisfying, and a decent night's rest.

These revelations rendered certain aspects of my life uncomfortable. I was beginning to recognize that my ethical framework did not jibe in any way, shape, or form with the Hollywood world into which I had sought entry. I knew now why I had no desire to be promoted. I even remember trying to visualize where I would be in twenty years. I remember thinking, *I don't want an Oscar. I don't want an Emmy. And I don't want a Grammy. If you don't want to be the best at something, what's the point?*

I was also discovering through my boss's relationship with the Democratic Party that Hollywood, much like the media, was part of the same architecture that Rush Limbaugh described. This boss, who shall remain nameless, was not an inherently moral individual. Everything that he did—*everything*—was about business. His devotion to wining and dining top elected Democratic officials was no exception.

Meanwhile, for the first time, through my autodidactic cycle of talk radio and books, I began to feel like an engaged adult. The homework that I abhorred in college—the dreary books, the nihilistic musings of dead critical theorists that had me embracing an anti-intellectual lifestyle—was being replaced by a new world of books and authors of whom I'd never heard.

My AM professors taught me to ask questions, to use the Socratic method. And I started to ask everyone around me some basic questions, but they didn't want to engage or couldn't engage in basic civil debate. The person that made this new pursuit of intellectual engagement invigorating and sexy was Camille Paglia. Her book, *Sexual Personae*, made me realize how little I really had learned in college. Her articles and assorted writings began to open my mind up to the fraud that is higher education in America. The origins of the problems in the media and in Hollywood begin in the sacrosanct, stultifyingly politically correct world of academia. It seemed to me that while Professor Limbaugh was focusing on the corrupt relationship between politics and the media and Professor Paglia was focusing on the corrupt relationship between politics and academia, I was beginning to hyperfocus, as we ADD types are apt to do, on the corrupt relationship between Hollywood and politics, and how academia, the media, and the political class conspicuously either ignore or denigrate all the ideas, authors, and voices that were now my lifeblood.

I was taking ownership of my own education. Words cannot describe the emancipation I felt to discard those confusing works and philosophers that my gut instinct had told me to reject. Nihilism, after all, is never a comforting companion. I had known it was garbage, but I felt that I couldn't tell a Harvard Ph.D. that I thought it was garbage. Surely my professors had known something I didn't. Now I was realizing that just wasn't true.

I guess it was inevitable that my relationship with my friend/high-IQ political guru, Mike, was bound for the rocks. Mike was someone else I had long believed must have known something I didn't. Around this time, Susie and I ran into him at Aron's Records in Hollywood one night. He was disoriented, confused, and incomprehensible. I followed him around the store trying to get his story before finally discovering that he was on mushrooms. This was when I recognized the distance that now separated us. What the hell is a grown man doing on a weeknight all by himself taking hallucinogenic drugs? I guess you can do that when you don't have a job.

Not long thereafter, when I would see Mike, I began to challenge him. I began to ask him questions. And I began to see that my Yoda was a bull-shit artist, had been all along. That he wasn't *borrowing* my CDs to tape them; he was taking them to the record store to sell to buy drugs. His philosophy, his poses, his trite, utopian, disapproving pronouncements—they were just boring. I stopped calling him, actually avoided him. And one day I got a phone call from a mutual friend who said Mike had been found murdered.

To this day, I hold great guilt that I did not cry when I heard the news. I didn't step through the normal Kübler-Ross stages of grief. But in Mike's life and in his death, I have ascribed to him an importance—he is my reminder, my personal cautionary tale. Mike's arrogant, elitist approach toward conservatism was laziness covered in pseudo-intellectualism. If I hadn't gotten out of New Orleans, I would have been Mike. He was the bullet I dodged, in every sense.

The world that I was now inhabiting demanded thinking, because it demanded results. My paycheck was a result. Susie's happiness was a result. Sleeping eight hours when it was actually dark out was a result. Paying my bills was a result. And buying the shoes that I worked in was a symbol that I had come so far in such a short period of time. I was becoming what my father, through his actions, taught me to become. I was becoming self-reliant and—gulp!—I was starting to come to the difficult revelation that I was a conservative...with the concurrent revelation that I wanted out of Hollywood. I was no longer going to four movies a week. I was no longer laughing the laugh track.

One day, without giving notice, I just walked out the door of my job and never went back.

Not long after, I was driving eastbound on Wilshire Boulevard at around Centinela one evening. I was overcome with the frustration that came from three excruciating years of postcollegiate learning—of trial and error, of a political and philosophical transformation in which something remained missing. I was twenty-five years old, had walked out on my only career prospect, and I had no friggin' idea what I was going to do with the rest of my life.

I'm not the most religious guy. In fact, at the time, I considered myself an atheist. But that pent-up frustration caused me to say aloud, in my car, "Please, God, give me something to do that I'm passionate about. Please give me a mission."

CHAPTER 3

Thank God for the Internet

I first heard of the Internet from a close high-school friend, Seth Jacobsen.

Over the years in prep school and college, my greatest coping mechanism was aligning myself with straitlaced, smart guys. Before a test I hadn't prepped for, they could always be relied upon to give up a quick view of their notes, which would push me into the C category. At the time, that was enough. Now here I was, after college, looking for the crib notes for life.

Seth was an Astrophysics major at Harvard (yes, he's that smart), and when I visited him for a brief weekend in 1989, I found out that some people actually studied at college. So when Seth came to my apartment in 1992 to tell me of a pending technological revolution, I was uniquely, perhaps pathetically, positioned to listen.

Seth said eight words to me that changed my life: "I've seen your future and it's the Internet."

I answered as any normal person would have in 1992. "What's the Internet?"

He started to explain to me what the Internet was, what HTML was, and why it was all a perfect fit for my ADHD. He made the World Wide Web sound like the Wild West in outer space, a romantic new frontier. I was fascinated. It was like I had just been shown the road map to my life. The only problem was that I had no idea how to read the map.

At that point, I had AOL and Prodigy and Compuserve. I was instinctively drawn toward these new services, even though I didn't know their endgame. But I knew I could get sports scores and make my own travel arrangements—basically, it just felt edgy and cool to be part of a medium where you could interact on a computer.

Around 1993, another friend, Dave White, lent me a copy of *Wired* magazine, which had just come onto the market. He had learned from *Wired* how to hook his computer up to the Internet, and he had started messing around with online groups like the Well. These were online communities, the precursors to chat groups. I was living below Dave in an apartment complex and working with my primitive technology, and I would visit Dave and watch his forays into the Internet's earliest incarnations and think to myself, *That's it. That's what Seth was talking about. And I'm eventually going to go there.*

In those days, it was complicated to get onto the Internet. The technology was so raw, the interface required programming knowledge to interact. It was the days when you had to type in "RUN" and operate the computer through MS-DOS. Compared to now, it was like using an abacus to do your tax forms.

But it was cool and exciting just the same. Seth had planted the seed, and I knew that for me, this was it. I'm only grateful now that I somehow realized it.

It wasn't until I was living in Austin, Texas, in 1994 (don't ask) that I finally sought out an Internet service provider (ISP) called Illuminati Online. Illuminati was somewhat famous at the time for a civil liberties case that it had fought and won. I tried to hook up to it, but had no luck—it was crazily complicated to try to get my computer to relate to my modem in order to connect to the Internet. The whole concept was just not idiotproof enough for me yet.

Then, one night, I decided that I was going to do it once and for all. I went to Central Market, a proto–Whole Foods on steroids—the Eighth Wonder of the World, an affirmation of capitalism deceptively marketed to guilty liberals—and bought a rotisserie chicken and a six-pack of Pilsner Urquell. And I sat down at my glorious Mac and said to myself, *I'm not going to leave this room until I'm on the Internet.*

I huffed and puffed through hours of trial and error, over and over, with no hint as to whether I was even making any progress. It was like trying to reach the finish line of a marathon in a thick fog. But then, surrounded by gnawed chicken bones and empty beer bottles, I heard the vital crackle of the modem connecting. And instead of it breaking off, the connection stuck.

I was reborn.

The Internet in those days was a free-for-all libertarian haven. I saw, even at the very beginning, that this was a new medium born of unwieldy individualism, of people who so desperately wanted to communicate with the world outside of the Democrat-Media Complex (whether they were aware of that construct or not), that they sought each other out in this technological wilderness. I recognized that for the Internet to exist, and for people to have such a massive desire to get on it, there had to be a driving force—and that driving force was the suffocating ubiquity of the Complex. Here was a place where freedom of speech truly existed, where you could say anything, think anything, be anything. It was no wonder that the first adopters of the Internet were the outcasts of the Complex: libertarians and conservatives.

But it still had some basic problems. When I discovered the Internet, I needed it to be *faster*. Seth was right—my ADHD-tempo mind needed information fast, fast, fast, with no delay. I turned the "Images" function off the browser so that slow-loading GIFs and animations wouldn't monopolize my surfing time. Even though I didn't have a lot of money then, I hated the slowness of the Internet so much that I bought an ISDN line for my apartment. It was an extravagance, in hindsight—nobody else had an ISDN line. I didn't care—the 28K-baud slowness of the Internet was making me insane.

But the slowness of the Internet at the time had an upside for me. Because I needed the information all the time, without pictures—I needed text—I found the alt newsgroups. I was soon obsessed: alt.current-events.clinton.whitewater, alt.showbiz.gossip, alt.fan.artbell, alt.fan.farrahfawcett, and a bunch of others. The Clinton alt group was my favorite, and it really exemplified what the early Internet was all about.

There were two regulars who were really vocal on the alt.Clinton group. One was some guy named Wayne Mann, who hailed from a place called Arroyo Grande. I signed up for his e-mail list. Every day, he would send out these massive e-mail files of articles that compiled all the data that was available about Clinton, whether related to Whitewater or Casa Grande or any of the other myriad scandals cropping up around Bill and Hillary at the time. For every possible Clinton scandal, Mann was accumulating information and then distributing that information. It was obsessive and incredibly detailed, a political digest with one focus. Taking into account the number of recipients of this information this one guy had signed up by e-mail, it seemed just an unprecedented operation.

The other person dropping his ideas into this alt group (and many others) was somebody named Matt Drudge. He had a news digest he called the Drudge Report. It wasn't a single-issue focus like Mann's—it was more one person's exotic mishmash, his vision of what the news world was or should be. Drudge would have articles about the latest political scandal alongside articles on the upcoming election right next to articles on behind-the-scenes Hollywood business news, undercover contract talks, early revelations of box office data...all juxtaposed with earthquake and hurricane data. It was like a tour of one man's short-term memory.

Perhaps because of the inherently hyperactive nature of the report—being able to jump pell-mell from one short news item to the next—it was the Drudge Report that really grabbed me. I read it and I read it and I read it every day. It wasn't hard to find: it had been posted in virtually every alt group I visited. It was just fascinating, unique, and worldly, while also being oddly uncynical.

Maybe it was this lack of cynicism that most captured me. My generation had embraced Kurt Cobain and late-1980s stand-up comedy and *Spy* magazine—we'd embraced irony as our badge of hipness. And for some reason, I was getting over it. It was weird—I was usually the best in the room at using that weapon, was comfortable being Joe Irony. But it was just starting to bore me. I was sick of the same sitcoms, I was sick of the same songs, I was sick of the same cookie-cutter everything. I felt myself moving past this defensive irony, toward that least hip of beliefs: values. With the Drudge Report and the Internet, I thought, *Here, at least, is something that takes itself seriously.* I was gaining nourishment from something outside of humor and cynicism; I'd found that reading about big issues and listening to other people's thinking about conservative ideas and morality and societal standards was actually fulfilling.

I guess I was looking for authenticity, and when I started reading Drudge's stuff, it rang in a more authentic and original voice. He mashed together extreme weather with Jerry Seinfeld's request for a million dollars per episode with the announcement that Bob Dole was going to pick Jack Kemp as his running mate (Drudge broke that story), and it was just interesting—it seemed to just capture the culture, the zeitgeist, so well. And that was the underlying feel, that this was a guy who was interested in the world and in life, and that the world and life weren't sucky, cold, and depressing, but in reality they were endlessly fascinating, and worth reporting on and talking about.

At the very end of the digest on the alt group website was a link that said, "Click here to subscribe." I clicked on it and started receiving Drudge's digest in my e-mail inbox. The digest also had a link to his website: www.lainet.net/drudge (don't bother searching for it—it's been wiped away by the sands of time). That alone showed his creativity. In those days, when you got your first ISP, one of their gimmicks was to give you five megabytes of disk space to create your own webpage. Drudge's personal webpage was the Drudge Report, which was a supplement to the newsletter he was sending out (remember, this was when "the Internet" didn't just mean the World Wide Web). It was a creative use of a free space.

At the time, my process of morphing into a conservative was being spurred on by talk radio and a new reading list; I was just discovering something unique about myself. For me to realize that there was another voice out there, and that he was doing something about the stranglehold of the Complex, was a revelation. Reading the Drudge Report was opening my eyes to the power of the individual to take on massive, entrenched power—in government, the media, everywhere. To borrow a phrase: Drudge was hope and change.

Then, on July 4, 1997, Drudge broke the Kathleen Willey story. "Coming just hours after the President 'adamantly' denies harassing Paula Jones," wrote Drudge, "the DRUDGE REPORT has learned that NEWSWEEK ace investigative reporter Michael Isikoff is hot on the trail of a new development that threatens to ignite premature holiday fireworks at the White House. Reports have surfaced that Isikoff has been in contact with a former White House staffer who may offer 'pattern' evidence of improper sexual conduct on the part of the President."[1]

Willey, a Clinton donor's wife, claimed to have been fondled by the president when she went to visit him—and when she got home, she found that her husband had killed himself. The Willeys were

having financial trouble, and so it was natural for
the Willeys to approach Clinton. And because
Clinton is who Clinton is, it was just as natural
for Clinton to allow the meeting, because Kathleen
Willey was an attractive woman. While Willey was
there and in the process of telling Clinton that
she and her husband were in deep financial straits,
the classy gentleman that Clinton is allegedly put
the moves on her in a special kitchen area off the
Oval Office. According to Willey's later interview
on *60 Minutes*, Clinton "kissed me on my mouth
and pulled me closer to him. And...I remember
thinking— ...'What in the world is he doing?' He
touched my breasts with his hand...and he
whispered... 'I've wanted to do this ever since I laid
eyes on you.' And...then he took my hand, and he
put it on him."[2]

A story that went all the way to the White House.
Broken on Drudge. It was mind-boggling to watch
how one outsider was frazzling the whole order.

A couple months later, on August 31, 1997,
Princess Diana of Wales was killed in a car crash
in the Pont de l'Alma tunnel in Paris. Drudge had
the story up with the iconic "Drudge siren" on his
site before cable news and the networks, in their
frantic Paris- and London-based coverage, reported it.

The string of successes of man vs. media was

starting to add up. Tons of media began profiling Drudge, the Internet started gaining attention as something other than a hobby, and—naturally!—members of respected journalistic institutions began slandering Drudge with charges they couldn't back up, let alone prove.

He was not just a threat to the political order—he was also a threat to the business of the mainstream media.

By the summer of 1997, I had actually struck up something of an acquaintance with Drudge over the Internet, and it was in fact he who hooked me up with Arianna Huffington. Arianna had become interested in creating media-driven websites, and she was looking for help from someone who knew the landscape. So I went to her house, and we sat outside and ate spanakopitas and drank iced tea. I'd read about Arianna in *Vanity Fair*, and I thought she was one of those people who was larger than life, the type of person nobody like me gets to meet. She was already writing a column for the *Los Angeles Times*, the *New York Post*, and the *Chicago Sun-Times*. Before I could even get comfortable being in her picture-perfect estate, accepting her graciousness, eating her hors d'oeuvres, I was abruptly hired.

I immediately quit a disposable E! Online job,

which I had gotten from the classifieds, and where I had spent most of my time teaching myself the technical basics of the Internet (the job also gave me access to their T-1 line, the equivalent of the Autobahn for the Internet in 1997). I guarantee you, E! did not lament losing a key cog in their machine. I had learned all I needed to do basic HTML, and I thought, *Okay, I know what I need to know, and now I'm going to create websites for Arianna and see where it takes me.* With less than a formidable arsenal, I was about to become a website designer.

I'd be working out of Arianna's house in Brentwood, not far from my apartment in Santa Monica. It fit my lifestyle all the way down to the bizarre and cloistered office she provided for me, which was hidden behind a huge painting. It was like a secret panic room situated above her office, accessible only by a spiral staircase, and which itself looked just like an old English study in the board game Clue.

The first day on the job, I went into her office and she sat me in front of her desk. She handed me a piece of paper that said on the top "Director of Research." It had a small list of job requirements.

I asked, "What is this?"

She countered, "Which of these things can you do?"

I didn't get it. "You want me to find somebody to become your researcher?"

"Just tell me what you can do on this list."

The first requirement was the ability to type. "I'm a hunt-and-pecker."

She said, "That's okay."

Requirement two: ability to write. "Okay," I said, "I wrote for my college paper and a couple of local entertainment magazines."

"Yes, darling, perfect."

Requirement three was the ability to edit. "Uh, I guess," I said. "I mean, I don't know those weird book editor symbols, but I know basic grammar."

At this point I was getting a little confused. I'd signed up to create websites for a rich, conservative columnist and speaker, an easy job, and now this was feeling like a bait-and-switch.

But before my confusion could turn into anger, I saw requirement four: "Do you know how to use LexisNexis?"

And it hit me between the eyes that for all of my stumbling and bumbling, I had tripped over the perfect job for an Internet information junkie. LexisNexis was the key to satiating my cravings, a database aggregating virtually every article in the modern history of media, both mainstream and obscure. For a person organizing bookmarks of every newspaper, who wanted to find every piece of information that was out there, LexisNexis was the Holy Grail. This was before Google, and you can find a lot on Google today—but even now, Lexis-Nexis is the greatest thing in the world, and having access to it was a dream come true.

I'd never felt so good to be duped in my life. At twenty-seven—gulp!—I felt like I might actually have the first job I wanted to keep.

Then it got even better. Arianna next informed me that there was a story she was working on, and that the source of the story was staying in her house while she wrote the piece. The source's name was Norma Nicolls, and she was the personal secretary to a man named M. Larry Lawrence.

Larry Lawrence was the owner of the Hotel del Coronado in San Diego, and he became the top donor to Bill Clinton; he was therefore rewarded with the ambassadorship to Switzerland. From 1991 to 1996, Lawrence gave $200,000 to Democrats. At the time, the world was just finding out the list of favors the Clinton White House was paying out for high-end donors, including overnight stays in the Lincoln Bedroom. A cursory investigation into Lawrence's background showed that he had some suspect business relations in Detroit. Already I was getting excited—this was fun, interesting. The layers of intrigue to the story involved sex, politics, and Bill Clinton, one of my personal chosen online investigative obsessions.

When Larry Lawrence died of cancer in 1996, Bill Clinton provided him a waiver to be buried in Arlington National Cemetery. He was the first Merchant Marine to be given this sacred honor. In the 1990s, Larry and his fourth wife, Shelia, had spent a lot of their time running around to Merchant Marine and Clinton fund-raisers, giving their money and hoping to get goodies back in return. Goodies, apparently, like being buried in Arlington National Cemetery sacred land.

But that wasn't the real story. The *real* story was that Larry Lawrence wasn't even a Merchant Marine.

Norma Nicolls told Arianna that back in the early 1990s, Lawrence asked her to research the history of the Merchant Marine at a San Diego library. Then, Nicolls said, Lawrence started writing checks to the Merchant Marine. All of a sudden, the Merchant Marine started giving him awards, because he was giving them money. He started claiming that he had served aboard the USS *Horace Bushnell*, a Merchant Marine ship torpedoed during World War II, and that he had been thrown into the Arctic Ocean as the ship sank.

And Arianna was onto both scams: Clinton's culpability in selling an Arlington burial slot, and Lawrence's culpability in falsifying a pseudomilitary record in order to gain entrance.

On November 24, 1997, Arianna started revealing the story to Americans:

> The more we delve into Larry Lawrence's last years, the more he looks like the poster child of President Clinton's Make-A-Wish Foundation for big-time donors....
>
> Lawrence's only military link was his service in the Merchant Marine during World War II. "I was surprised and disturbed," Norma Nicolls, his executive assistant from 1979 to 1993, told me, "to learn that Larry was allowed to be buried at Arlington. I was a Navy officer's wife for 24 years, who lost many good friends in the Vietnam War. I believe that should be a privilege accorded only to those who have given up something for their country. I worked as his personal assistant for almost 15 years before he was appointed ambassador to Switzerland, and as far as I know, he never expressed a desire to have a military funeral."
>
> It appears that the driving force behind the effort to bury Lawrence at Arlington was his fourth wife, whose petit-bourgeois appetite for honors and distinctions seems to have no limit. Whatever the truth about his Merchant Marine service, can anything—other than political services rendered—explain multiple medal win-

ners standing in line awaiting admittance to Arlington while Lawrence is allowed to cut ahead? Way ahead.[3]

The response was swift and brutal from the mainstream media. Maureen Dowd, a charter member, ripped Arianna, writing in her syndicated column, "The Clintonites have hidden behind double-talk so often, it was tempting to believe the Republicans' sinister allegations. But the GOP case began to melt.... What you need to know about the Republicans is that the charge was disgusting."[4] White House special counsel Lanny Davis told the press that Lawrence "was thrown overboard and suffered a serious head injury. Had he been in the Navy and the same incident would have occurred, he would have received a Purple Heart." The late Richard Holbrooke, former assistant secretary of state, said, "I'm dumbfounded that there would be the slightest question about the appropriateness of Larry Lawrence being buried at Arlington." Army Secretary Togo West said there was no political motivation to Lawrence's burial. "I am the responsible person.... Just not done. Not possible...He deserves to be there."[5]

But Arianna was just getting started. She was responding to attacks on her credibility with calm and composure, knowing that she had the goods, and reacting with utter serenity as she watched a phalanx of media swarm around her, looking for their pound of flesh. She fed them the story, bit by bit. And I was helping. There was a moment in my research when I personally realized that everything Arianna was saying was true. I was spelunking and spelunking, and finally I came across something big. I ran down to Arianna's office yelling: "Arianna, Arianna! He didn't serve in the Merchant Marines. I'm positive." It was a piece from the *San Diego Union-Tribune* dated January 19, 1993. The story talked about how Lawrence had been honored by the Merchant Marine at a dinner, where he had recalled "the morning when, as an 18-year-old, he suffered head wounds during a German torpedo attack on his ship in the frigid waters off Murmansk." There was only one problem: according to the newspaper, the incident was "previously unknown to most of his family and close friends." To me, that was the whole goods. It was the confirmation in my mind that everything Arianna was laying out for the American public was true.

Arianna ran with it. Citing that piece and responding to her critics, she wrote, "What about the fact that the *Horace Bushnell's* manifest does not include Lawrence's name? Or the fact that the casualty list for the ship also has no record of the injuries so movingly described by the White House counsel? Indeed, according to the Maritime Administration and the U.S. Coast Guard, there is no record of Lawrence having served in the Merchant Marine at all."[6]

The house of cards that the Complex constructed for Larry Lawrence began to crumble. The same media that had attacked Arianna now began to swing behind her, calling for Lawrence's disinterment from Arlington: folks like Sam Donaldson, Cokie Roberts, George Stephanopoulos—and yes, Maureen Dowd. All I could say as I watched it was three words: "This. Is. Awesome."

The awesomeness culminated on a Thursday morning in December. I was working in my hidden office when I heard Arianna shouting: "Come down, come down, come down!" I came downstairs, and she pointed at the TV and shouted, "Watch!"

CNN was on. And it was showing aerial helicopter footage of Arlington National Cemetery, where a series of banquet tents formed a labyrinthine path to the exit of Arlington. They were disinterring Larry Lawrence at the behest of Shelia Lawrence, Larry Lawrence's aforementioned fourth wife, who, along with Clinton's liberal media allies, had shot at Arianna without aiming first in an attempt to smear her. They had instinctively defended Larry Lawrence. They had put their names and credibility out there, and when caught red-handed, none of them had ever apologized. But it didn't matter. Arianna was staring at the TV with a look of utter serenity on her face: she'd gotten her scalp.

I knew right then and there that I needed to find a way to do this for a living.

One night in late December 1997, I watched an episode of *Nightline*. The subject: Matt Drudge. The premise: an entire hour about Matt Drudge. They started with this: "Do you know who this man is?" A picture of Drudge at his computer flashed on the screen—type, type, type. "If you don't, you soon will." The show actually went on in a semipositive vein—as positive as you can get for a conservative with a few scalps, a conservative who is trailblazing against the Complex. They had the requisite slams, of course, posting a picture of Drudge's website next to pictures of extreme websites, implying that the Internet was filled with crazies and white supremacists. But for the most part, it was fair.

Little did I know that ABC News was foreshadowing something much greater than Kathleen Willey or the death of Princess Diana.

They were foreshadowing the demolition of a presidency.

*   *   *

In January 1998, I was a happy guy. I was happily married, living in a tiny house with (I swear) a white picket fence. I had my buddies Arianna and Matt, and we were all hanging out together, and we were all doing more from Los Angeles with minimal resources than the mainstream media were doing from Washington, DC, with hundreds of reporters. It was great fun.

About two weeks after the New Year, on January 16, 1998, I spent the day at home paying attention to the unprecedented deposition Bill Clinton was giving due to his former student, Judge Susan Webber Wright, ruling that he had to testify in Paula Jones's civil lawsuit. For me, as a Clinton aficionado, this was a huge day—a sitting president testifying about accusations of sexual harassment.

Now, I was against overly broad sexual harassment law on a philosophical level because of my belief that feminism had defined sexual harassment down to the type of interaction that created so many marriages—a secretary and a boss meeting each other at work, for instance. I didn't believe in the post-structural PC Marxist/feminist critique that said that sexual relationships were inherently relationships between the oppressor and the oppressed, and that power structures between bosses and employees necessarily rendered such relationships a form of sexual harassment. I thought that was nonsense, which is why Clarence Thomas's confirmation hearings had been such an epiphany for me. But at the same time, I knew that if they were going to hold Thomas to that standard, they had to hold Clinton to that standard as well.

The Clinton hearings became, to me, the living embodiment of the Democrat-Media Complex—and the inherent biases of the media were multiplied when cable news came of age during this era. With an enormous dedication of resources, the Complex went to work spinning Bill Clinton out of peril.

Watching a purported women's-rights advocate get away with sexual harassment—shoving cigars in the help, groping job applicants in the hallways—was the emblematic example of the media double standard, where a liberal could get away with anything as long as he toed the politically correct line. Clinton could attack women, use his gun-toting state troopers to recruit hand-picked groupies for him as if he were a rock star, pull down his pants and say, "Kiss it." He could get away with it because he was a liberal, and because liberals wanted him to get away with it. I wanted Clinton to pay, and I wanted his enablers to pay—I wanted to see them held to the standard that they had created to destroy their enemies.

I wanted Clinton to get busted because it was obvious to me that this was the type of person you would not let your daughter date, your sister date, any distant relative date—that this was a guy who was not virtuous, that he was a glutton, that he had a voracious appetite for power and women and food and anything that he could use to fill himself up. As a human being, he was essentially a sociopath, but the mainstream media had built him up because he possessed weapons that suited their purpose: the correct pro-abortion and left-of-center economics policies, the wily charms of a born cad, and a venal commitment to the politics of personal destruction.

After watching the hearings, at around midnight, I got home and started to climb into bed. Before I did, I logged on to the Internet. In my e-mail box was the Drudge Report.

NEWSWEEK KILLS STORY ON WHITE HOUSE INTERN, the all-caps headline bannered. BLOCKBUSTER REPORT: 23-YEAR OLD, FORMER WHITE HOUSE INTERN, SEX RELATIONSHIP WITH PRESIDENT.

At the last minute, at 6 p.m. on Saturday evening, NEWSWEEK magazine killed a story that was destined to shake official Washington to its foundation: A White House intern carried on a sexual affair with the President of the United

States! The DRUDGE REPORT has learned that reporter Michael Isikoff developed the story of his career, only to have it spiked by top NEWSWEEK suits hours before publication. A young woman, 23, sexually involved with the love of her life, the President of the United States, since she was a 21-year-old intern at the White House. She was a frequent visitor to a small study just off the Oval Office where she claims to have indulged the president's sexual preference. Reports of the relationship spread in White House quarters and she was moved to a job at the Pentagon, where she worked until last month. The young intern wrote long love letters to President Clinton, which she delivered through a delivery service. She was a frequent visitor at the White House after midnight, where she checked in the WAVE logs as visiting a secretary named Betty Curry, 57. The DRUDGE REPORT has learned that tapes of intimate phone conversations exist....

Michael Isikoff was not available for comment late Saturday. NEWSWEEK was on voice mail.

The White House was busy checking the DRUDGE REPORT for details.[7]

* * *

I got into bed and stared at the ceiling. "Holy shit," I said. "He did it."

I was surprised to find a tear running down my face. I turned to Susie, who was lying beside me.

"Susie, history just happened," I murmured. "Drudge just changed everything."

CHAPTER 4

Hey, Old Media: It's Not Your Business Model That Sucks, It's *You* That Suck

On February 19, 2010, I spoke at the Conservative Political Action Conference (CPAC). The day before I spoke, Kate Zernike of the *New York Times* reported on another panel at the conference. In particular, she wrote about a young author and investigative journalist named Jason Mattera: "How can conservatives win the youth vote that overwhelmingly went for Barack Obama in 2008? At the Conservative Political Action Conference, apparently, some are betting on using racial stereotypes." What had Mattera done? He "mocked what he described, with a Chris Rock voice, as 'diversity,' including, he said, college classes on 'cyber feminism' and 'what it means to be a feminist new black man.'...Offering up a slogan, he adopted the Chris Rock voice again: 'Get your government off my freedom!' "[1]

Except that Mattera wasn't doing a Chris Rock impersonation. He was doing a Brooklyn accent— *because he's from Brooklyn.*

So when I spoke later that day, I called Zernike out by name. "Kate Zernike of the *New York Times*, are you in the room? Are you in the room? You're despicable. You're a despicable human being." Then I said what I really feel about the media: "This is what these creeps do. I'm sick of having cocktails with them. I'm now at war with them. No more cocktails."

I'm at war with the mainstream media because they portray themselves as objective observers of reality when they're no such thing—they're partisan "critical theory" hacks who think they can destroy everything America stands for by standing on the sidelines and sniping at patriotic Americans with all their favorite slurs. They have nothing but contempt for the American people. They use all the weapons they have at their disposal to intimidate every one of us and force us to shut up and not to speak our minds.

Their days of doing this are over. They're dying because they hate much of America and what it has historically stood for. Then they moan that no one wants to consume their product, saying it's their business model that has just sold them short.

News flash to the media: *It's not your business model that sucks. It's you that suck.*

* * *

My biggest experience yet with the mainstream media came after Drudge broke the Monica Lewinsky story.

As much as Lewinsky was a story, the story behind the story was the media's determination to scuttle it as fast as possible. *Newsweek* had already tried to shut down Isikoff. The Friday before Drudge unleashed the scoop, *Newsweek* told Isikoff they might not run the story at all: "The first signal I got that the story might not go was when I was told we need a backup story on Clinton's Paula Jones deposition in case we don't go with the story," Isikoff said later. Isikoff himself was concerned about the ramifications of releasing the story, since even the single Linda Tripp tape he had in his possession was supposedly "ambiguous. It neither confirmed nor undercut the most serious charge, that the president and Vernon Jordan, Clinton's trusted friend and adviser, instructed her to lie. That was the serious federal crime that [Special Prosecutor Kenneth] Starr was investigating. The tape that we heard, which was only one tape, did not prove that." *Newsweek*'s managing editor, Mark Whitaker, blamed killing the story on the fact that the Starr team hadn't yet grilled Lewinsky: "Let's say they came back and said, 'We talked to her, she denied everything. We believe her.' Or they said,

'We questioned her. She sounds like a flake. We are dropping the whole investigation.' Then we would have been irresponsible to write a wildfire story about sex in the White House." At 4:45 p.m. ET on Saturday, Editor in Chief Richard Smith said that *Newsweek* was going to hold the story pending further investigation.

All of this reeked of Clinton-defending, even the tone of the comments. Whitaker characterized the Lewinsky scandal as "a story about sex in the White House," which it wasn't—it was a story about the president of the United States committing perjury. Isikoff was acting as though journalistic standards were the same as jury standards—beyond a reasonable doubt, when he could simply have run with the story and let the world know that there were tapes of a White House intern talking about giving the president of the United States blow jobs in the Oval Office. That's a story in itself.

The Clinton-defending carried over the next morning on ABC's *This Week* with Sam Donaldson. *Weekly Standard* editor Bill Kristol brought up the story on the panel, freaking out everybody else there: "The story in Washington this morning is that *Newsweek* magazine was going to go with a big story based on tape-recorded conversations, which a woman who was a summer intern at the White House, an intern of Leon Panetta's—"[2]

Immediately, ABC commentator and former Clinton flack George Stephanopoulos jumped in, stating that the Drudge Report had been "discredited." This was a position crafted by the Clinton White House—Stephanopoulos had in fact called up the White House that morning and spoken with John Podesta, Clinton's chief of staff, who told him, "The only way you can respond to it is to say, 'This is Drudge, he's a rumormonger...and you can't believe what you read in the *Drudge Report*."[3]

Kristol responded, "No, no, no! They had screaming arguments in *Newsweek* magazine yesterday. They finally didn't go with the story. It's going to be a question of whether the media is now going to report what are pretty well-validated charges of presidential behavior in the White House—" At which point Sam Donaldson intervened and said that he didn't think anyone should comment on the Drudge Report story until *Newsweek* had a chance to explain why it killed the story.[4]

It was typical baffling-with-bullshit from the Democrat-Media Complex. Stephanopoulos, by the way, has now been rewarded by ABC News, his employer, with the false label of a neutral, objective reporter—not once, but twice—for thwarting legitimate stories. Early in the 1990s, Stephanopoulos acted to prevent the #1 *New York Times* bestselling author Gary Aldrich from talking about what life was like coordinating FBI efforts to vet employees under Clinton. (Aldrich basically said it was like trying to vet a druggie fraternity house—a test I would have failed, but then, no sane person would have nominated me.) Sam Donaldson was saying it wasn't even worth discussing until *Newsweek* got a chance to explain itself. The Democrat-Media Complex protects its own—and in the case of Stephanopoulos, it rewards former political hacks with journalistic firewall status. They get to pretend to be independent-minded people while actually acting as barbed-wire fences protecting their masters from insurgent campaigns from the right.

With *This Week*, the blackout had begun. Doyle McManus, Washington bureau chief of the *Los Angeles Times*, said, "I looked at [the Drudge Report] and thought, 'If Isikoff wants to pursue that story, he's welcome to it.'"[5] On CBS's *Face the Nation* and NBC's *Meet the Press*, lawyers appeared to talk about Paula Jones's legal strategy—and nobody mentioned the Drudge story. Tim Russert refused to touch it because, "There's not enough there." He asked James Carville, Clinton's attack dog, whether there was "a pattern of behavior that those who support President Clinton are worried about?" then allowed Carville to respond, without rebuttal, "The president denies it, and...frankly, I know the president's telling the truth." That evening on CNN, the lead story was Clinton sexually harassing...Kathleen Willey, a story that was six months old. Carole Simpson on ABC's *World News Tonight* led off with the story that Paula Jones was skipping out of DC. Sam Donaldson, the Clinton defender, spun the Clinton deposition as a Clinton win, somberly intoning, "Behind the scenes, the spinning of the story continued. Paula Jones and her group dined Saturday night with champagne, professing to be pleased with the way things had gone. Friends of the President one-upped that by telling *Time* magazine the Clinton camp is ecstatic about the way the deposition went."[6]

The media ran from the story in one mass stampede.

And the next night, at 11:52, Drudge released Lewinsky's name.

And for the next day and a half, the media maintained their silence. Finally, on Wednesday morning, perhaps sensing that with the name out there the dam would burst soon, the *Washington Post* ran a story. The *Los Angeles Times* followed suit. At 8 p.m. on Wednesday night, Michael Isikoff's four-thousand-word piece on the Lewinsky scandal posted at *Newsweek*'s website—or rather, at the AOL website, since *Newsweek* still didn't have its own website.[7]

By the time the media finally broke their blackout, it had been all day Sunday, all day Monday, and all day Tuesday. That was *four days* of the story existing in the undermedia—the Internet and talk radio—and Drudge reporting on the story one bit at a time, giving more and more evidence, messaging, "We've got the goods." Even as the media were finally starting to recognize the story, Drudge was breaking new ground. That Wednesday, he ran a headline: REPORT: LEWINSKY OFFERED U.N. JOB; INVESTIGATORS: DNA TRAIL MAY EXIST. And just to stick the knife in, he added the notation, CONTAINS GRAPHIC DESCRIPTIONS. The report revealed that "investigators have become convinced that there may be a DNA trail that could confirm President Clinton's sexual involvement with Lewinsky…. Tripp has shared with investigators a conversation where Lewinsky allegedly confided that she kept a garment with Clinton's dried semen on it—a garment she said she would never wash!"[8]

It was a media frenzy by now. Four days after the story broke, and after thinking the story had been killed by George Stephanopoulos, Hillary Clinton had to appear with Matt Lauer on the *Today* show to try to put the scandal to rest. On January 27,

1998, an unnaturally balanced Matt Lauer grilled Hillary Clinton over her husband's reported indiscretions. First she blamed the "vast right-wing conspiracy" to get her husband. Lauer asked her whether the charges "came as big a shock to you as anyone." The rest was history:

Hillary: And to my husband. I mean, you know, he woke me up Wednesday morning and said, "You're not going to believe this."

Lauer: And so when people say there's a lot of smoke here, your message is…Where there's smoke…

Hillary: There isn't any fire.

Lauer: If an American president had an adulterous liaison in the White House and lied to cover it up, should the American people ask for his resignation?

Hillary: Well, they should certainly be concerned about it.

Lauer: Should they ask for his resignation?

Hillary: Well, I think that if all that were proven true, I think that would be a very serious offense. That is not going to be proven true.[9]

But there wasn't just smoke. There *was* fire. It wasn't just a triumph for Drudge. It was a triumph for the truth-seeker seeking to challenge the insurmountably complex media behemoth that, over time, had tried to kill a legitimate story for political purposes. Drudge leaked it little by little by little. And when they started to attack him over the course of the next few months, that was when Drudge dropped the cigar story as a "fuck you" to the Democrat-Media Complex. On August 22, 1998, Drudge bombshelled, SHE HAD SEX WITH CIGAR: MEDIA STRUGGLES WITH SHOCKING NEW DETAILS OF WHITE HOUSE AFFAIR. Again, he headlined that the story contained graphic descriptions. "In a bizarre daytime sex session, that occurred just off the Oval Office in the White House, President Clinton watched as intern Monica Lewinsky allegedly masturbated with his cigar. It has been learned that several major news organizations have confirmed the shocking episode and are now struggling to find ways to report the full Monica Lewinsky/Bill Clinton grossout."[10]

Clinton's carefully crafted media defense was going down, and Drudge was dismantling it as brilliantly as anyone in media history.

But the Democrat-Media Complex isn't enormously powerful because they give up easily. Over the course of the next eight months, they took an open-and-shut case of sexual harassment, of perjury, of intimidation of witnesses—they took that epic slam-dunk and used a coordinated media propaganda campaign of monumental proportions to split the country apart. They went after all their political enemies to try to draw blood regardless of what the infraction was; they used the media, a critical part of the Complex, to legitimate it. Over the next eight months, I learned all I needed to know about the ethics of journalism. The rules were created by the left to be applied exclusively as a weapon against the right.

For the next eight months, the Clinton administration and their media parrots devised a strategy that assessed, through polling, every possible aspect of the story.

They asked the American people: "What do you feel about the intimidation of Monica Lewinsky and Linda Tripp not to testify truthfully in the Paula Jones civil trial?"

"We don't like that."

"What do you think about the president lying under oath?"

"We don't like that."

"What do you think about the president lying to Donna Shalala and the rest of his cabinet?"

"We don't like that."

"What do you think about the exploration of the president's sex life?"

"We don't like that."

"Aaaaah," said the Democrat-Media Complex. "Good! There's our wedge."

They crafted a wedge from Clinton's sex life and they went to their messengers in the intellectual circles to shove that wedge between Americans' shoulder blades. They knew that most Americans still thought that Clinton was a liar and a sexual predator, but they knew that if they could only convince Americans that "everybody lies about sex," everything would turn out fine for their man, no matter how hypocritical and manipulative they were being to save him.

They started with the classic leftist tactic: the politics of personal destruction applied to Lewinsky. This effort was spearheaded by Sidney Blumenthal, a former mainstream media journalist. According to Christopher Hitchens, who testified before Congress in 1999, Blumenthal attended a Washington luncheon soon after the revelations broke, at which "Mr. Blumenthal stated that…the President was 'the victim' of a predatory and unstable sexually demanding young woman." In other words, Blumenthal used his Rolodex to distribute the dirt that the reason Bill Clinton was in the proximity of Monica, with whom he "did not have sexual relations," was because she was a stalker.[11] In fact, Blumenthal used the word *stalker* several times during a March 19, 1998, luncheon at the Occidental restaurant in Washington, DC, explaining that "this version of the facts was not generally understood."[12]

Blumenthal later blamed Lewinsky herself for this version of the story; in his book *The Clinton Wars*, he stated, "Beginning with Isikoff's publication of the Talking Points on January 21, in which Lewinsky called herself a 'stalker,' newspapers around the country and all the television networks and cable stations expanded upon the stalker theme."[13] Except that only Blumenthal took that claim seriously enough to actually label Lewinsky a stalker in the menacing rather than colloquial sense. According to Hitchens, Blumenthal told Hitchens's wife that he only gave credence to the "stalker" account because "the President told me." He then followed up that stunning admission with an even worse admission: "I could go to jail for what I'm doing now."[14] Apostates like Hitchens are given the most egregious treatment by the Complex; the Clintonistas labeled him a drunk and a traitor to the cause.

The next step was for Blumenthal to recruit some of his intellectual friends to write that the Republicans were somehow engaging in a "sexual inquisition," despite the fact that it was Clinton who had made the details of his sexual peccadilloes relevant by committing perjury about them. Blumenthal instructed friends of Clinton's to write long pieces that all had the same meme: that the repressed conservatives were obsessed with a president who had a "European" view of sex. These pieces opened the door for the academic and pop-cultural worlds to begin echoing the slogan: "It's just about the sex."

One of Blumenthal's buddies was Colombian Nobel Prize–winning novelist Gabriel García Márquez. On January 30, 1999, García Márquez penned a piece for the UK *Guardian* defending Clinton. The title of the piece: "Why My Friend Bill Had to Lie." García Márquez began by discussing Clinton's magnetism, then his status as a cultural icon: "At 49, he was a glorious survivor of the generation of '68, someone who had smoked dope and sung along to the Beatles, someone who had taken to the streets in protest at the Vietnam war." What any of this had to do with Clinton ejaculating his DNA into and onto a White House intern was left unspoken.

At last, García Márquez tackled the question of the hour: why did Clinton have to lie? Clinton had to lie, García Márquez said, because, as Clinton himself told García Márquez, "My only enemy is right-wing religious fundamentalism." Then García Márquez got into full bore: "Is it right that this exceptional human man should have his place in history distorted because he couldn't find a secluded spot in which to make love?...The President only wanted to do what the common man has done behind his wife's back since the world began. Puritan stupidity did not only refuse him that, it withheld his right to deny it." But what of his perjury? García Márquez dismissed it out of hand: "Surely it is more dignified to perjure yourself in defence of carnal desire, than to condemn love altogether?"

Clinton was innocent, said García Márquez. The right wing was to blame, "because Puritanism is an insatiable vice that feeds off its own shit. The entire impeachment process has been a sinister plot by fanatics for the personal destruction of a political adversary whose grandeur they could not bear." According to García Márquez, Clinton's enemies were straight from Hawthorne's *The Scarlet Letter*. And not only that—they were secret racists! "Toni Morrison, a Nobel Prize winner and one of the greatest writers of this dying century, sums it up in one inspired flourish. 'They have treated Clinton as if he was a black president.' "[15]

García Márquez was just one of Clinton's "highbrow" defenders recruited by Blumenthal. Another was Alan Dershowitz, who wrote an entire book defending Clinton, entitled *Sexual McCarthyism*. On NBC, he said, "Remember, it was sexual

McCarthyism that J. Edgar Hoover used to try to get Martin Luther King." William Styron, author of *Sophie's Choice*, focused on the sophisticated European reaction to the Lewinsky scandal: "I have been very intent on the reaction of Europeans, and they are almost uniformly devastated by this. They realize how deadly serious it is." Jack Lang, former French minister of culture, joined the club: "Tyranny begins when one power, one church, one party introduces itself into the private life of its citizens."[16]

The coincidence of messaging was too perfect not to be orchestrated from the top. This had been a story about Clinton lying to the American people, forcing witnesses into silence, and breaking faith with the constitutional order. Now it was a story about evil Republican oppressors with secret sexual issues trying to drag Bill Clinton's open-minded sex life out of the closet and thrust it upon the American people. Suddenly, Clinton was a hero, and the Republicans trying to impeach him for high crimes and misdemeanors were the villains. It was brilliant.

To this point, the media were doing what they had always done. Though left of center historically, they did have some boundaries of civility. But now, in 1998, the Clinton administration, through its attempts to save a presidency at any and all costs, experimented with the New Media, particularly the well-funded, San Francisco–based upstart Salon.com. There, government and a publication with nothing to lose—and an ideological kinship—conspired to do things that were previously considered off-limits.

It started with the Clinton apparatchiks hiring private detectives to dig up information about their political enemies. In February 1998, private detective Terry Lenzner, along with Blumenthal, was subpoenaed before a federal grand jury for trying to find damaging material on Kenneth Starr's prosecutors. Clinton's attorneys acknowledged that Lenzner was on their payroll. In Washington, he was called the head of "Bill Clinton's private CIA."[17] Kenneth Starr, who stayed admirably quiet during the entire Clinton investigation, released a statement: "This office has received repeated press inquiries indicating that misinformation is being spread about personnel involved in this investigation. We are using traditional and appropriate techniques to find out who is responsible and whether their actions are intended to intimidate prosecutors and investigators, impede the work of the grand jury, or otherwise obstruct justice."

Naturally, Lenzner played victim, and the White House, according to the *New York Times*, "denounced the questioning of Mr. Blumenthal and

Mr. Lenzner as a vindictive campaign by Mr. Starr and his deputies to intimidate the President's aides and associates and to chill the White House's relations with the press. White House officials assailed Mr. Starr's efforts to force Mr. Blumenthal to reveal his contacts with reporters as an assault on the Constitution." Rahm Emanuel—yes, that Rahm Emanuel—came to the defense of All the President's Thugs, jabbering, "There is no legal right he will not trample on in his partisan political pursuit of the President. When we have seen this abuse of power in other countries, we have been outraged. When you see it at home, you are left speechless. It is brazen abuse."[18] Nobody in the media thought to ask whether it was brazen abuse to hire detectives to pressure prosecuting attorneys.

This, of course, was common practice for the Clintons. The Clintons had at one time or another hired Terry Lenzner, private eye Jack Palladino, and private eye Anthony Pellicano to do this kind of dirty work. Pellicano had allegedly been hired by Hillary in 1992 to discredit Gennifer Flowers. Palladino had been used to silence women during the campaign; the Clinton election committee paid him $93,000 to "investigate" the women. According to Betsey Wright, one of Clinton's aides, Palladino even went so far as to create "an affidavit or two" linking Flowers to a conservative conspiracy.[19]

It wasn't surprising that the Clintons were able to come up with mud on their political opponents. Blumenthal then disseminated that information through his Rolodex as fast as he possibly could. Once they got to the bottom of the barrel in terms of mud, though—once they got to the material that no responsible editor could ever justify as mildly relevant to anything, the material that they couldn't go to the *Washington Post* or the *New York Times* with—the Clintons went to their alternative medium.

That alternative medium was Salon.com. The same Salon.com that is based in San Francisco, the Salon.com where all the editors knew the strategies of the alt weeklies I had read back in Venice—the "outing" and the politics of personal destruction. They knew those strategies because they *were* those strategies.

It was Salon.com that first reported on August 5, 1998, that the Clinton administration was going to employ a "sexual scorched-earth plan.... Die-hard Clinton loyalists are spreading the word that a long-ignored but fearsome tactic has now resurfaced as an element in the President's survival strategy: The threat of exposing the sexual improprieties of Republican critics, both in Congress and beyond, should they demand impeachment hearings in the House. 'We're talking about the Doomsday

Machine here,' one close ally of the President told Salon, alluding to the unstoppable chain of retaliatory nuclear strikes in the movie *Dr. Strangelove.* 'Once the Doomsday Machine is set in motion, there will be no stopping it. The Republicans with skeletons in their closets must assume everything is known and will come out. So the question is: Do they really want to go there?' "[20]

On September 16, 1998, David Talbot, a Hollywood kid (his father, Lyle, headed up the Screen Actors Guild) and San Francisco journalist, ran a story on Salon.com about Rep. Henry Hyde, head of the House Judiciary Committee. The story had nothing to do with Hyde's qualifications. It had to do with an affair Hyde had had thirty years before with Cherie Snodgrass. Talbot made clear that Hyde was being "outed" as a decades-old adulterer because "Hyde's committee will decide whether the adulterous affair President Clinton carried on with a White House intern, and his efforts to keep it hidden, should be referred to the House of Representatives for impeachment proceedings." Hyde admitted the 1965–1969 affair to Salon.com, but pointed out how irrelevant the story was to anything at issue in the Clinton investigation: "The statute of limitations has long since passed on my youthful indiscretions…. The only purpose for this being dredged up now is an obvious attempt to intimidate me and it won't work." Salon.com even tracked down Cherie's adult daughter, who made clear that she was speaking out because of Hyde's role in the Clinton impeachment: "My mother originally didn't want me to say anything to the press. But she's just so fed up with [Hyde], with how two-faced he is.... She hates his anti-abortion stuff, and all the family values stuff. She thinks he's bad for the country, he's too powerful and he's hypocritical."[21]

The editors at Salon.com knew that the Hyde story was totally extraneous to the Clinton situation, and that it was a gratuitous smear designed to get Hyde and the rest of the constitutionally mandated impeachment managers to back off Clinton and, more important, to intimidate others from pursuing an honest outcome. Because Salon.com was flacking for the Clinton White House and appeared to be getting their scoops from them, they felt it necessary to disassociate themselves so that Clinton wouldn't feel the blowback: "The White House had nothing whatsoever to do with any aspect of this story. We did not receive it from anyone in the White House or in Clinton's political or legal camps, nor did we communicate with them about it." *Sure.*

The truly incredible part of the Salon.com editorial was its explanation of *why* it would release the information. Where the mainstream media had turned it down flat—even they wouldn't stoop this low, at least not yet—Norm Sommer, the supposed source of the scoop, had tried to pitch the story to the *Los Angeles Times*, the *Boston Globe*, and the *Miami Herald*—Salon ran with it. The question, again, was *why*. "In a different and better world, we would not have released this story. Throughout the tragic farce of the Clinton-Lewinsky scandal, we have strongly argued that the private lives of all Americans, whether they are public figures or not, should remain sacrosanct…. But Clinton's enemies have changed the rules. In the brave new world that has been created by the Clinton-Lewinsky scandal, the private lives of public figures are no longer off limits," the editors wrote. This was patent nonsense, of course. If Salon wanted the private lives of public figures to remain private, the worst way to achieve that was by releasing the private details of Henry Hyde's thirty-years-past sexual liaisons.

The real reason was easy: Salon released the information in order to decimate Clinton's detractors. Salon's editors explained on the site: "Aren't we fighting fire with fire, descending to the gutter tactics of those we deplore? Frankly, yes. But ugly times call for ugly tactics. When a pack of sanctimonious thugs beats you and your country upside the head with a tire-iron, you can withdraw to the sideline and meditate, or you can grab it out of their hands and fight back."[22]

With Salon.com tearing the lid off of a can of Ebola bacteria, the *Hustler* publisher Larry Flynt got busy, too. The year before, Hollywood had produced an ode to Flynt starring Woody Harrelson, *The People vs. Larry Flynt*, which had antihero Woody telling America, "I think the real obscenity comes from raising our youth to believe that sex is bad and ugly and dirty. And yet it is heroic to go spill guts and blood in the most ghastly manner in the name of humanity. With all the taboos attached to sex, it's no wonder we have the problems we have. It's no wonder we're angry and violent and genocidal."

So Larry Flynt, now somehow a First Amendment icon getting a pass from the ladies of NOW, decided on October 4, 1998, to offer $1 million to anyone who would reveal damaging sexual information about congressional Republicans in an ad in the *Washington Post*. His purpose was to defend Clinton, just like his friends and allies at Salon.com. "No matter what channel I turned the television to, it was Bash Clinton Night," Flynt wrote in his autobiography, *Sex, Lies & Politics: The Naked Truth*. "Everybody wanted his head on a platter and I thought it was grossly unfair. He hadn't robbed the country's treasury. He hadn't committed treason. At worst, he got a blow job in the Oval Office, and like any married man caught under those circumstances, he lied to cover his ass."[23]

Larry, in full political operative mode, went on: "We received some very colorful leads that we ended up not pursuing," he wrote in 2004, "because our interest was exclusively in finding and exposing the hypocrites. I wasn't interested in trashing somebody's sex life just because they were having an affair or they were into something kinky. I only wanted to expose people who were…crucifying Clinton for doing the same thing they were."[24]

The first person Flynt exposed was presumptive Speaker of the House Bob Livingston (R-LA), who Flynt revealed had serially cheated on his wife. *Roll Call* (the Capitol Hill newspaper) picked up the story right away.

Next was Rep. Bob Barr (R-GA). Flynt said that Barr had paid for his wife's abortion and committed adultery. Barr had never denied committing adultery, but he did deny that he had encouraged his wife to have an abortion. Flynt said that Barr had committed perjury, too—except that Barr had refused to answer questions, which is not the same as committing perjury. Barr's scandal was covered everywhere.

As this tactic gained momentum, the mainstream media finally decided it was safe to get on board. Rep. Helen Chenoweth (R-ID) admitted to the *Idaho Statesman* that she had had a longtime sexual relationship with an associate named Vernon Ravenscroft. For being totally unjustifiable as a news story, this was probably the most egregious of these so-called exposés. Chenoweth was single and she wasn't a member of Congress when she had the sexual liaison. Salon.com chortled, "To her regret, she discovered that making your private morality a story by questioning the President's is a really bad campaign idea."[25]

Rep. Dan Burton (R-IN) outed himself—he had fathered an illegitimate kid in the 1980s—in order to avoid being targeted by *Vanity Fair*. As Salon.com triumphantly wrote, "Unnerved by the thoroughness with which independent journalist Russ Baker and others have been probing his apparently active life, Burton outed himself. Believing Baker's piece was going to be in the upcoming *Vanity Fair*, Burton decided to cryptically pseudo-confess a slew of past sins with a kind of preemptive strike."[26]

Americans thought all this was disgusting, just like I did. A poll in the *Washington Post* showed that only 40 percent of Americans approved of Flynt's mission to reveal "extramarital affairs by Republicans." Fifty-seven percent disapproved. Only

46 percent of Americans said the mainstream media should report such scandals, with 52 percent saying no.[27]

For the Complex, this campaign was the John Philip Sousa "Stars and Stripes Forever"—the end of the fireworks display on the Fourth of July, when you hear *pop! pop! pop!*…except that when you looked around, you saw bodies strewn all over the place, the bodies of conservatives, and every one of their closeted peccadilloes smeared across their corpses. I looked around and said to myself, *What the hell just happened?*

The Republican Party itself refused to acknowledge that it was happening. While the countermedia—the Drudge Report and Lucianne Goldberg and Rush Limbaugh—were leading the charge against the campaign, the Republicans, except for those few people who went about their business pursuing the articles of impeachment, ran for the hills. The institutionalized conservative movement and specifically Newt Gingrich were conspicuously silent. They knew they were in no position to be going after Clinton for impeachment, even though it was on legal grounds, because they had allowed the left to turn the media narrative into one of sexual inquisition. They didn't want to put themselves in harm's way. The people pushing for impeachment were like today's Tea Partiers, men and women who were pushing their representatives, telling them over and over again, "No, you guys have to have courage, and if you're going to be in the battle, you have to know you're going to take bullets, too."

It was watching the Republican Party run from their responsibility to their constituents in order to save themselves that caused me to cultivate a more limited respect for them. I looked at the one guy who stood up, knowing he'd be isolated, Rep. Jim Rogan (R-CA), and they decimated him even as Republicans fled around him. Rogan was the American dream—a guy who had spent time on welfare, who raised himself up and eventually ended up in Congress—and they destroyed him unmercifully. The Clintonistas, as they are commonly referred to for their revolutionary media battle tactics, put a hit out on Rogan, using outsized resources to target him in his next election. The payback is not just payback—again, it is a warning to anyone else that politics to these people is a blood sport and if you cross them, you will pay dearly. This was when I recognized that the next Republican president was going to be isolated for attack. The message was that the Complex still controlled the big guns, and if you punched them, they'd punch back twice as hard. George W. Bush's fate was preordained.

✳   ✳   ✳

To the nation, the media's Clinton-created response to the Lewinsky scandal was a turning point. They had been the Edward R. Murrow wannabes, the guys who idolized Woodward and Bernstein. Now they were open partisan hacks digging up as much dirt as possible, whenever possible.

That became even more clear to me two years later, when, absent the "ugly times require ugly measures" excuse, Salon.com ran a piece by Dan Savage, the radical gay-left columnist from the Pacific Northwest. Savage infiltrated then–presidential candidate Gary Bauer's Iowa campaign at the caucus level and, under the guise of being a conservative Christian, got a job for one month to help out.

Savage described how, sick in bed watching television, he'd devised his plan. Watching Bauer on MSNBC, he saw Bauer state, "Our society will be destroyed if we say it's okay for a man to marry a man or a woman to marry a woman." It isn't exactly news to those of us who have lived outside San Francisco that religious conservatives feel this way.

But it was news to Savage:

In my Sudafed-induced delirium I decided that if it's terrorism Bauer wants, then it's terrorism Bauer is going to get—and I'm just the man to terrorize him. Naked, feverish and higher than a kite on codeine aspirin, I called the Bauer campaign and volunteered. My plan? Get close enough to Bauer to give him the flu, which, if I am successful, will lay him flat just before the New Hampshire primary. I would go to Bauer's campaign office and cough on everything—phones and pens, staplers and staffers. I even hatched a plan to infect the candidate himself.... My plan was a little malicious—even a little mean-spirited—but those same words describe the tactics used by Bauer and the rest of the religious right against gays and lesbians.

He spent the rest of the piece describing with glee how he applied his bodily fluids to the entire office—he licked "the front door, office doors, even a bathroom door...the staplers, phones and computer keyboards...the rims of all the clean coffee cups drying in the rack." Then he chewed on a pen and handed it to Bauer.[28]

This is not journalism. It's not even the third-grade ramblings of a snot-nosed booger eater. It's the vicious actions of a perverse, degraded, and disgusting human being. And Salon ran it without question. Why? "It was savage (no pun intended), powerful writing, Swiftian in its desperate, satiric outrage at anti-gay discrimination."[29] In other words, the ends justify the means.

This was Salon.com. It wasn't like this was an alt weekly with ads for hand jobs. For many people, this was a respected publication. That these people allowed for such a story to be published, sending the message that it was open season on Christian conservatives, without so much as a *Columbia Journalism Review* symposium labeling such behavior outrageous and asking how best to shame Salon for so completely abandoning journalistic standards...it was a new low. If a conservative writer had done the same thing to a Democratic candidate, that writer would not only be shunned—he'd need a criminal defense attorney.

I believe strongly that this was the moment in which the politics of personal destruction—especially in the age of New Media, where the Old Media were on their way out—took over the business. The *New York Times* and *Time* and *Newsweek* were all finally figuring out that they were clinging to each other in desperation as they plummeted off the financial cliff. Their downfall was the result of their failed business model combined with their failed ideology. But their foot soldiers were now firmly embedded in the New Media, where the left's partisan hackery could operate on a whole new front. Drudge had taught them the power of the Internet. Now, with all its collusion and single-minded advocacy intact, the Complex was firmly established on this new frontier.

It was all about to reach the breaking point with the election of George W. Bush.

CHAPTER 5

The Democrat-Media Complex Strikes Back

I had watched Bill Clinton get his hand stuck in the cookie jar (or in a humidor, to be more precise), and I had watched the forces of the New Media hold him accountable in a way the Old Media would not. I had also studied the perfection of the politics of personal destruction under the Clintons. In particular, I witnessed a shameless president turning the national tragedy of the Oklahoma City bombing into a political opportunity to attack a personal enemy. Before the real culprit, Timothy McVeigh, was even arraigned, Clinton had blamed talk radio (read: Rush Limbaugh) for fomenting the climate that led to this isolated incident. It was disgusting. And it was effective.

By 2000, I knew these people inside and out. I knew how they operated all too well.

Early in that election cycle, I spoke with John Fund of the *Wall Street Journal*, sensing that the Clintons had crafted the plan to control the Democratic National Committee by putting lackeys like Terry McAuliffe in charge. Sensing also that they were looking for revenge after the New Media had maligned and nearly destroyed the Clinton presidency, I predicted that their strategy would be to isolate somebody for destruction as a cautionary tale to conservatives. Clearly targeted were those on the right who had been emboldened by the emergence of talk radio and the Internet as communications tools for the masses. The message sent to the New Media conservatives would be clear: you punched us, and we will punch you back twice as hard.

"George W. Bush," I said to John, "is making a huge mistake with his 'uniter not a divider' line." Using his lieutenant governor—Bob Bullock, a Democrat—as a campaign prop in order to demonstrate his goodwill was a mistake. Establishing the standard that he was the good guy who could work with the other side? A mistake.

"It's a mistake because they're going to use that 'uniter not a divider' line as a means to mock him and pillory him, undercut his affability and his frat boy good nature, his charming-nickname-for-everybody-in-the-room style," I told John. "They're not going to grant him his legitimacy; they're not going to grant him his humanity. They're going to take his personable friendliness—his biggest skill set—and turn it against him. They're going to try to destroy George W. Bush. We are about to witness one of the greatest assaults on an individual in the history of the country."

It started right from the beginning. Even before Bush stepped into office, the left used Florida as its first launching pad. The Gore people picked their targets: Bush, Dick Cheney, Katherine Harris. Mark Fabiani, a Gore adviser, told the *New York Times* candidly: "We needed an enemy."[1] It was raw hysteria plus total media conformity. It didn't matter that Bush won Florida by every possible count, and it didn't matter that even the *New York Times* and *USA Today* and every other major publication ran stories tabulating the "uncounted" votes and recognizing Bush's victory (on page 16B, by and large). What mattered were the front-page stories emphasizing that Gore had won, Bush had stolen the election, and the Supreme Court was in the pocket of the big corporations that wanted their man in the White House.

Bumper stickers appeared reading "Not My President" and "Selected, Not Elected" and "Don't Blame Me, I Voted for Gore." The academics all rallied around the cause. Princeton University professor Fred Greenstein labeled Bush a cowboy moron who had no basis for governing as a conservative: "Bush is very good at claiming victory. He has a 'Marlboro Man' approach to communication. His idea of having a mandate is to say 'I have a mandate.' "[2]

After the Supreme Court rightly ruled that arbitrary ballot counting was unconstitutional, the New York Times put the opening stamp of disapproval on the Bush presidency before it had even begun, holding Bush's feet to the fire on bipartisanship and claiming that Bush would have to abandon his political principles in order to attain legitimacy: "To make deals with the Democratic leadership in Washington, the President-elect is going to have to bridge some ideological gaps. But this seems to us a time to take Mr. Bush at his harmonious word.... A Presidency that starts out under a cloud of doubt can transform itself into a success at the vital center of politics, where most Americans would want it to be."[3]

As the new president entered the White House without the usual bipartisan grace notes from the losing side, the exiting Clintonistas vandalized many of the offices they were vacating and, in an act of pure spite, removed the W from computer keyboards. Bush, the uniter, refused to pursue the matter. Eventually, of course, Bush would learn too late that magnanimity was not a winning strategy against this crowd.

The first eight months of the Bush presidency were spent by the New Media fighting to rebuff liberals of all ilks: pundits, writers, commentators, all arguing that Bush had stolen the election and that this wasn't a real presidency and that he was just plain stupid. While the Clintons properly fought to lay the predicate that their daughter, Chelsea, was off-limits—John McCain was rightfully chastised for an uncalled-for and cruel joke at Chelsea's expense—the same press immediately targeted the Bush daughters for ridicule. The press pursued Jenna in particular and framed her as a wild party child, and even Hollywood stars Brad Pitt and Jennifer Aniston took to *Rolling Stone* magazine to make Jenna the butt of an unfunny joke.

The same Larry Flynt who had spent hundreds of thousands of dollars attempting to tear down Republicans to save Clinton called Bush "the dumbest President we have ever had." Martin Sheen, who many in West Los Angeles thought was the real president because of his role on *The West Wing,* called Bush a "moron." Michael Moore predictably stated, "Once you settle for a Ronald Reagan, then it's easy to settle for a George Bush, then it's real easy to settle for Bush II. You know, this should be evolution, instead it's de-evolution.

What's next?" Flynt, Sheen, and Moore never graduated college (Flynt didn't even graduate high school).[4] Bush graduated from Harvard Business School.

Maureen Dowd, whose writing can be buoyant and insightful, picked up the "Bush is stupid" mantra in her column immediately after Bush's election. Commenting on President Bush's visit to Yankee Stadium in May 2001, Dowd wrote, "Some days, it's fun to be the boy toy of the military-industrial complex.... Doesn't W. realize that EVERYBODY in the world HATES us?...Gerhard Schroder thinks that he and W. had no communication when they met, and that W. had trouble remembering his name. Tony Blair has to call Bill Clinton to find a sympathetic ear." She accused Bush of "trying to turn Alaska into a giant oil rig and give more riches to the rich." She accused him of "rewarding his contributors with the Pentagon."[5] There's that bipartisan feeling Bush was talking about!

They were well on their way to destroying Bush.

Then 9/11 happened.

September 11 obviously changed everything. It stopped the left from bleeding the country dry with its cynical partisanship veiled as "objective" and "neutral" coverage and commentary. The liberal model of separating Americans into different categories as a means toward empowering group leaders to tell their followers what to think, what to believe, and how to fight everyone else was over. They couldn't pit Americans against each other anymore, and that scared the hell out of them, because that was how they'd gotten themselves elected for decades. September 11 took the pendulum and swung it away from polarization and toward unity; it brought America back to its natural state of *E Pluribus Unum* for a very short time, a time in which even Democrats were awkwardly forced to hold hands with Republicans and sing "God Bless America."

Nothing was clearer to me at that time than the artificiality of the feeling, the fact that Democrats were caught in an unpredicted, unpredictable moment in which their tactics for gaining and holding power and manipulating situations were frozen solid. They didn't know what to do. They didn't know how to handle things, because it had been a lifetime since the honest Democratic Party was taken over by the far-left operatives.

Into that void stepped George W. Bush. He acted as a real leader, and he brought the country back together. He was no-nonsense, and he wasn't the cowboy the Complex had made him out to be. "When I take action," he said on September 13, 2001, "I'm not going to fire a $2 million missile at a

$10 empty tent and hit a camel in the butt. It's going to be decisive."[6]

When he spoke on September 20, 2001, the Democratic angst was already evident that this president had beaten their politics of personal destruction. "Tonight, we are a country awakened to danger and called to defend freedom," Bush said. "Our grief has turned to anger and anger to resolution. Whether we bring our enemies to justice or bring justice to our enemies, justice will be done." And as Bush spoke, the camera panned to Senator Hillary Clinton—a woman President Bush had greeted with a warm hug in the Oval Office just a week before, after the attacks—and Hillary was sitting there and her arms were folded tightly. It was such a telling moment, because Hillary isn't like Bill, with his shit-eating grin, his good ol' boy charm. She's a bad actor. And you could tell right away that her well-funded, well-oiled, John Podesta–led machinery was of no use to her at a moment when Americans were connected like never before, when wedges were blunted and impotent.

The Democratic Party, which had put on a face of TLC moderation during the Clinton years, which had been headed up by the greatest triangulator and faux-moderate in American history, had painted itself into a corner. It was one thing for

Americans to embrace the soft socialism of the Democratic Party and their hatred for the American military when we were in the context of a peace dividend, when foreign policy was considered of secondary importance. It was okay during the 1990s that the Democratic Party had an obvious disposition against a strong foreign policy, and that but for Joe Lieberman and a very few others, the people in the Democratic leadership were primarily motivated by concerns of "social justice" and economic equality—socialism in everything but name—and that they wanted to decrease funding for the military because they were naïve doves. But when 9/11 happened, the Democratic Party's position became untenable—it granted the Republican Party a default dominant position in perpetuity if national security and terrorism were going to be the top story of our time.

So for a time, the Democrats stayed silent. In fact, just for show, they rallied around Bush. The *New York Times* reported, "Many Democrats who once dismissed Mr. Bush as too naïve and too dependent on advisers to steer the United States through an international crisis are now praising him and his advisers' performance. Some are even privately expressing satisfaction that Mr. Gore, who tried to make his foreign affairs expertise an issue in the campaign, did not win."[7]

That created an obvious vacuum for the left. The Democrats were too busy pretending to like Bush and a strong America to soldier on. The vacuum was filled by the extreme left, which would include groups like MoveOn.org and ascendant left-wing group blog the Daily Kos. I witnessed that process beginning to take shape around September 20, at the Los Angeles Federal Building, which is just south of my house. I walked down there with my family, and I saw all of the placards that four years later became mainstream slogans, pushing the politics of personal destruction against George W. Bush. These were radical leftist movement people, people aligned with Marxist pro-Stalinist organizations like International ANSWER, whose antiwar marches were unchallenged by a pliant media. Why the pass when it was clear that if the KKK had organized an antiwar rally, there would have been major media blowback?

I remember looking at Susie and saying, "This is going to be the resurgence of the professoriate and the Baby Boomer left. This is what they've been waiting for. This is going to be their last stand to fulfill their self-appointed '60s revolutionary mission."

They had been gathering. They had maintained their existence within the protective walls of college campuses. Their gray ponytails got more gray as time went on, but they never shed their belief systems. If you walked through the hallways of UCLA and looked at the professors' and lecturers' doors, you would have known they were still true believers in the 1960s world, and that they had allies in positions of power in unions all over the country and in Hollywood. These were people who had never met an antiwar storyline they didn't love. An alliance of preexisting, seemingly marginal, left-of-center remnants of a bygone era simply walked through the front door and took over the Democratic Party. The marginal political world of the alt weeklies that I used to read had taken center stage.

And I knew the tactic they were going to use: the media. They were going to aim the pop culture at selected MTV youth, Abercrombie & Fitch youth, brandishing antiwar bumper stickers and T-shirts. They were going to imitate the means and methods of the '60s. They were going to use their propaganda techniques, their stronghold in popular culture.

Hollywood led the way—that was a natural. They did it with a two-pronged strategy: they lampooned Bush, and they accused the right of attempting to silence them. (This while they wouldn't shut up about their supposed lack of free speech.) Celebrities spoke first, because when 9/11 temporarily distracted us from our pop-cultural obsession, they, narcissists that they are, demanded the limelight back, and anti-Americanism and left-wing slogan-eering became their de facto script for the Bush years.

Hollywood is a leftist colony. It was easy for Hollywood people to be the first "brave voices" to say "politically unpopular" things on soapboxes because their jobs were protected, because their bosses believed what they believed in. After 1972, in which Richard Nixon won and George McGovern lost (a fact Hollywood never really accepted—the late *New Yorker* columnist Pauline Kael said she couldn't believe Nixon had won, since everyone she knew had voted for McGovern), America sent a message to the left: we're not interested. So Hollywood decided to send a message to the country. The natural aging process was culling out patriotic Hollywood, with John Wayne and Gary Cooper dying and Jimmy Stewart coming to the end of his career, and the paradigms of the Western and the pro-war movies were giving way to the anti-Vietnam consensus. The counterculture took a foothold in the '60s in Hollywood, with the radical leftists inside the business taking over completely. They didn't just take over the business— they took over the art, infusing movies and television with antiheroes instead of heroes: *Easy Rider* instead of *Casablanca*, *Midnight Cowboy* instead of *The Man Who Shot Liberty Valance*.

Growing up in Hollywood—going to school there, where my administrators invited Tom Hayden to come speak without the slightest concern that many in the country considered him a traitor for legitimate reasons—I knew these people. They were my friends' parents, who voted for Hayden even though they owned million-dollar houses. These people, who hung out with the richest of the rich, gave license to their sense of entitlement and noblesse oblige by hanging out with political radicals while simultaneously wearing the outfits and haircuts of conformists. They started to sneak into traditional society pretending they were something they weren't.[*]

They were the first to start raising the anti-Bush flag once more. This was *long before* the Iraq War. They were concerned first and foremost with tearing down this rube, this symbol of American exceptionalism and unity.

The Iraq invasion took place in March 2003. In February 2002, just months after September 11 (Bush's approval rating was still around 80 percent at this point), TV's fake president Martin Sheen said, "George W. Bush is like a bad comic working

---

[*]Tom Wolfe famously wrote about this elitist poseurism in *Radical Chic & Mau-Mauing the Flak Catchers*, which, if you haven't read it, is a must.

the crowd, a moron, if you'll pardon the expression." George Clooney said in January 2003, "The [Bush administration] is run exactly like *The Sopranos*." Dustin Hoffman injected conspiracy-theory leftism in February 2003: "I believe that the administration has taken the events of 9/11 and has manipulated the grief of the country, and I think that's reprehensible." Robert Redford said something similar in December 2002: "Coyote? The group of 'em, a pack of coyotes—tricky, cunning, making sure to take care of themselves but doing it in a wily way, making sure they never get caught." Jessica Lange said in October 2002 while accepting a film award, "I hate Bush. I despise him and his entire administration. It makes me feel ashamed to come from the United States—it is humiliating."[8] Ed Harris went after Bush with a hammer and tongs: "Being a man, I have got to say that we got this guy in the White House who thinks he is a man, who projects himself as a man because he has a certain masculinity. He's a good old boy, he used to drink, and he knows how to shoot a gun and how to drive a pickup truck. That is not the definition of a man."[9]

Even as they pushed their hatred of Bush as fully legitimate and praiseworthy, the press did nothing. Actually, the press did worse than nothing—they gave them a microphone to distribute their views unchallenged. Susan Sarandon appeared on CBS's *The Early Show* and *Face the Nation*; Madonna appeared on *Dateline NBC*; Harry Belafonte appeared on *Larry King Live*, as did Sean Penn; Mike Farrell appeared on NBC's *Meet the Press*. As Laura Ingraham writes in her book *Shut Up and Sing*, "Whenever a top entertainer has a political bone to pick, he or she has an instant platform."[10]

Hollywood dragged out its oldest lefties and its youngest lefties. Jann Wenner, a Baby Boomer who still force-feeds the relevance of Bruce Springsteen with repetitive front-page power picks, used this movement to promote Green Day and any other pop-cultural vessel that would create antiwar albums. MTV found selective youth, sexy youth, wearing antiwar T-shirts, and put them on TV every night. There was an urge in Hollywood from the old and the young to affirm the Baby Boomer Boss-lovers' yearnings for the Age of Aquarius to be reborn in the Bush age.

These were the loudest people in the world. And the press was giving them free rein to say and do whatever they wanted, to incite political stunts reminiscent of the Merry Pranksters, to use media trickery to make points, to spawn a youth rebellion against the president of the United States during wartime. They were representing America abroad, and they were representing us as evil hayseeds bent

on killing brown people—and the media were abetting this slander.

Next, Hollywood engaged in a ploy designed to
paint the Bush administration with the tar of fascism—they accused Bush and conservatives of
shutting down their free speech. The juxtaposition
was astonishing—the false accusations that conservatives and Republicans were telling the left to
"shut up" alongside the simple fact that every burp
these bratty windbags uttered during this period
was printed and reprinted ad nauseam. But by accusing conservatives of McCarthyism and raising
that bugaboo, they wanted to do just what they
falsely accused conservatives of doing: they wanted
to shut them up.

As part of this, they crafted a "dissent is patriotic"
meme, an absurd slogan to begin with, that they
intentionally misattributed to patriotic Founding
Fathers like Benjamin Franklin (they would later
be forced to attribute it to pseudoscholar Howard
Zinn). Deconstructed, "Dissent is patriotic" is a
self-negating slogan because its validity clearly de-
pends on what kind of dissent you're talking about.
If you're a member of the neo-Nazis in America,
you're dissenting, but nobody would call that dissent patriotic. But if you're antiwar, dissent is auto-
matically patriotic, according to David Geffen's
guest list (even if you're a member of Al Qaeda,

presumably, since they are antiwar, at least as far as the United States goes). The aphorism is nonsensical. But the left repeated it so many times and so often that it lost all meaning. They slapped it on every bumper sticker on every Prius at every Whole Foods. And it worked.

Next, they accused conservatives of quashing this dissent. They framed their arguments as though they were victims, even while saying things that were outrageous and arguably un-American. Susan Sarandon said, "It's terrifying to me to feel the fear that exists now in the United States to even question anything for fear of being labeled anti-American."[11]

"The early signs are this administration could go further, shutting down information, not allowing certain truths to get out," said Robert Redford in January 2003. "And all you've got to do is look at history to see what that led to. The McCarthy era."[12]

In April 2003, Tim Robbins, Sarandon's former quasi–common-law husband and possibly potential corecipient of her Social Security check, famously warned of a "chill wind blowing in America." Where did he say that? At the National Press Club, of course, on national television as broadcast by C-SPAN. Why Robbins would be at the National Press Club to begin with is a question that, if you've made it this far in the book, I suspect you can reason out.

Robbins started off by telling the assembled media sycophants that after 9/11, he was ready for unity. What kind of unity? A unity where President Bush would use the momentum from 9/11 not to defend America, but to help people "at community centers to tutor children, to teach them to read...at old-age homes to visit the lonely and infirm...convert abandoned lots to baseball fields." Robbins's kind of unity "would send a message to terrorists everywhere: if you attack us, we will become stronger, cleaner, better educated, and more unified." Yeah, Tim, extending Head Start and giving funds to the local YMCA would have Osama bin Laden quaking in his sandals.

That unity didn't materialize, and Robbins knew it would never materialize, because nobody would seriously think that the Bush administration would fight terror with increased welfare payments. So Robbins turned against Bush: "In the 19 months since 9-11, we have seen our democracy compromised by fear and hatred. Basic inalienable rights, due process, the sanctity of the home have been quickly compromised in a climate of fear."

The only climate of fear was the one Robbins was generating, of course, but this new "climate of fear" allowed Robbins to pretend to be a victim: "A message is being sent through the White House and its allies in talk radio and Clear Channel [Communications].... If you oppose this administration, there can and will be ramifications. Every day, the airwaves are filled with warnings, veiled and unveiled threats, spewed invective and hatred directed at any voice of dissent."[13]

Robbins wasn't the only one pursuing this line of thought. The Dixie Chicks bashed Bush overseas and then complained about it on *Larry King Live* when people reacted with outrage, with Natalie Maines explaining, "I feel patriotic and strong. We will continue to be who we are." Sean Penn took out a full-page ad in the *Washington Post* in 2002, well before the Iraq War, in which he ripped President Bush for "[violating] every defining principle of this country over which you preside: intolerance of debate ('with us or against us'), marginalization of your critics, the promoting of fear through unsubstantiated rhetoric, manipulation of a quick comfort media..." Yes, Penn was a victim who could afford to take out a $56,000 ad in one of the nation's leading newspapers. (The best part of his ad was his suggestion that Bush "listen to Gershwin" in order to avoid war. Which Gershwin, exactly? *Porgy and Bess*? Or perhaps *An American in Paris*?)[14]

Even as the Hollywood left played the victim

game, they shut down members of their own community (or their perceived community) who disagreed with them. This is a town, after all, that boasts about Janeane Garofalo, who preaches, "Our country is founded on a sham: our forefathers were slave-owning rich white guys who wanted it their way. So when I see the American flag, I go, 'Oh my God, you're insulting me.' That you can have a gay parade on Christopher Street in New York, with naked men and women on a float cheering, 'We're here, we're queer!'—that's what makes my heart swell. Not the flag, but a gay naked man or woman burning the flag. I get choked up with pride."[15]

It's no wonder that conservatives in Hollywood are treated as though they suffer from highly contagious leprosy—and during the Bush years, that only escalated. They pumped out antiwar dud after antiwar dud, and they cast out every right-winger vengefully, or at least every right-winger they could find.

But the phenomenon wasn't limited to Hollywood; it was a pattern that pervaded the left. If you offended the prevailing sensibilities of your "group," you were made to pay. Joe Lieberman was a living example. He was savaged for dissenting on one issue at a time when dissent was supposedly patriotic, and at the same time the left was claiming false victimhood. The left painted Lieberman as the conscience of the Senate when he ran for vice president with Al Gore in 2000; now he was a traitor. He needed to be destroyed as a message to anyone who would actually dare to show true dissent. By 2006, Lieberman had been thrown out of the Democratic Party for his heresy and was now an independent senator from Connecticut.

Perhaps the best example, though—and one that played out in the New Media landscape—was Andrew Sullivan. Sullivan, an openly gay man, understands the penalties that go along with speaking out against the Complex if you're a member of one of the subgroups; if he were given truth serum, he'd have one hell of a story to tell.

Sullivan said he was a conservative in the 1990s and the early 2000s. More than that, he backed George W. Bush's election in 2000 because, as he put it, "when I look at what he is proposing to do, I agree with him far more than I do with Al Gore. For me to support Gore on his current big-government, leftist platform would simply mean renouncing most of the principles I have long believed in and cherish." Sullivan even went so far as to renounce identity politics: "I believe in an equal society with equal rights for individuals—not a balkanized society where membership in certain groups guarantees special privileges and rights." Even though he was for gay marriage, and even though Bush, as he said, "thinks gay people should live as criminals under sodomy laws (which is almost enough to send me back to Gore)," Sullivan realized that Bush "would represent an uneven and unprincipled check on the balkanization of America."[16]

In June 2001, Michelangelo Signorile, a gay journalist who specializes in the vile practice of "outing" prominent people with whom he disagrees, went after Sullivan with a pickax in the alt weekly *LGNY*, along with buddy Michael Musto from the *Village Voice* and David Ehrenstein from the *Los Angeles Times*. They found his personal sexual advertisement on a gay website, where he was looking for partners who were also HIV positive and didn't want to use condoms. He basically said in his ad that he liked it every way and liked to give it every way. And the gay left, which hated his endorsement of Bush, used it to embarrass him, ruin him, intimidate him.

Nonetheless, after September 11, Sullivan stood strong by Bush. On September 18, he wrote, "I am relieved that George W. Bush is President of the United States. I am more than ever proud of endorsing him last fall.... We have the right man in the job."[17]

Over the next two years, Sullivan maintained his

pro-Bush position, hoping to convince gay Americans that Bush's push for liberty in the Arab world was good for the gay community. Then, in February 2004, in response to the Massachusetts Supreme Court's ruling forcing same-sex marriage on the state, Bush came out in favor of a constitutional amendment to protect marriage. That was it for Sullivan. He went berserk. "WAR IS DECLARED," he proclaimed in CAPSLOCK. "Those of us who supported this President in 2000, who have backed him whole-heartedly during the war, who have endured scorn from our peers as a result, who trusted that this President was indeed a uniter rather than a divider, now know the truth."[18]

In his well-traveled, influential post-9/11 writing, Andrew Sullivan had two fronts: progay, and pro-war-on-terror against radical Islamists. Which meant he was living two lives. For years, Sullivan was effectively fending off the gay left. It was a tenuous, delicate détente in which Sullivan rightfully posited that Bush was fighting for Western liberalism over the blatantly antigay and medieval radical Islam. How Sullivan held the gay left at bay for as long as he did was impressive. But when Bush disappointed him by taking a stand against gay marriage in the strongest possible terms, Sullivan had a choice: either lose his standing in the gay world, or keep that standing and ditch Bush.

* * *

Aside from Hollywood and the gay left, the mainstream left began trotting out "victim" after "victim" to blame Bush for their misfortunes. The left began politicizing 9/11 by suggesting that if anyone from the right mentioned it, they were exploiting 9/11 in grotesque fashion, while simultaneously granting authority to the Jersey Girls, whose husbands died that horrific day and who blamed the Republicans (exclusively) for presiding over the eight months prior to 9/11, as opposed to the eight years of prior Democratic leadership in the White House.

The left also accused the right of the tactics they themselves were using, claiming the right was politicizing 9/11 and challenging the patriotism of its political enemies. Max Cleland was brought out as a symbol of his hero status, his legs missing, not to defend his point of view from a rational angle, but as an unassailable symbol of the left's invulnerability—if you attacked the left, you were attacking war heroes like Cleland. Cindy Sheehan came out of the woodwork and was granted automatic heroine status by the press (until she turned on the Democratic Party, at which point she was relegated to Crazyland).

All these tragic symbols were trotted out, one after another, in order to create a solid shield for the Democratic Party against the Republican Party's foreign policy approach. Meanwhile, the eunuchs in the Republican leadership allowed this campy, over-the-top theater to grab the moral high ground, even though it was espousing surrender in the war on radical Islam and the disembowelment of George W. Bush. The Republican leadership allowed the antiwar movement to become mainstream.

There were few who spoke up against this. Only Ann Coulter had the guts to take them on at the time. Ann had experienced the underhanded attention of the media left and refused to be defeated just because her opponents tried to destroy her. Her refusal to play by the enemy's rules made her a warrior of the highest order, exposing the leftist tactic of using grief as a means of stifling dissent. And even though the left threw every grenade in their arsenal at her, Ann shamed them into taking the Jersey Girls, Cleland, and Sheehan out of heavy rotation. She did so by pointing out that these "victims" were cynically being used as political weapons, and the charge was so obviously true it stuck. Coulter's acts are pilloried to this day, yet those same manufactured spokespeople and those tactics are conspicuously still out of commission. Politics is not for the faint of heart.

Ann's defiance and success taught me a valuable

lesson: the people most detested by the Democrat-Media Complex, the ones who are most marginalized, are the ones who are the most effective. At that moment in time, I started to realize that we needed to fight the leftist wave with all of our strength and all of the means at our disposal. They *can* be beaten.

Between the war in Iraq, the introduction of "victims" of a manufactured "intolerance" toward dissent, the ire and tactics of the gay movement, and the unyielding propaganda of the Hollywood left, all the strands braided together to form a leftist rope of monumental strength—a rope made to hang George W. Bush from the highest turret.

I watched with increasing trepidation the ultimate attack on Bush that I had previously predicted to friends and family. I watched the collective effect of the Hollywood class's reaction to 9/11, which consisted of splitting the country when we were united. And I decided to stop fighting behind coattails and to start fighting in my own name.

That's why, in 2004, I wrote *Hollywood, Interrupted* with Mark Ebner, a no-holds-barred underground Hollywood journalist. I wrote it out of the pure outrage welling up in me as I saw the Hollywood left filling the void in the Democratic Party after 9/11, normalizing the most extreme scorched-earth measures against a wartime president. I wrote it because of Sean Penn, and Martin Sheen, and all these radicals who had clean haircuts and wore three-thousand-dollar suits and used the power of their image to legitimize the profoundly damaging metamorphosis the Democratic Party was undergoing—the transition from the party of Joe Lieberman to the party of Nancy Pelosi, Harry Reid, and Howard Dean.

The biggest point I wanted to make was one I'm still making: *Hollywood is more important than Washington.* It can't be overstated how important this message is: pop culture matters. What happens in front of the cameras on a soundstage at the Warner Bros. lot often makes more difference to the fate of America than what happens in the back rooms of the Rayburn House Office Building on Capitol Hill.

That book covered everything from the sexual deviance of the Hollywood crowd (it was like Tulane West) to the cult adherence to Kabbalah and Scientology to the discrimination against conservatives in the business. It was a total assault on the town and on the industry.

It was also my first taste of personal public scrutiny. For the first time, I was a public figure appearing on Fox News and AM radio, not just to attack these people and their methods, but to remind Americans that Hollywood wasn't trivial—that it was the most dangerous propaganda tool of the left in America.

During that time, Dennis Miller began putting me on the air, and I started to realize the value of some of these tactics that the left uses. I saw the value of telling a joke while making a point. I was beginning to act on my theory that it was more important to stay in Los Angeles and effect change from the outside of Washington and the inside of pop culture rather than the other way around. I was beginning to understand how to integrate jokes and humor into a hybrid persona that was part politics and part entertainment.

But along with those realizations came another realization. I began to see the fundamental flaw in the left's scorched-earth tactics—they can only tear down, not build up. And it hit me that the tearing down of The Other wasn't enough. Every time I did a Fox News hit where I attacked Michael Moore, no matter how valid the attack, no matter how much I had raised my fledgling Q rating, I felt emasculated and cheapened because I was only tearing down, not building. I felt the inherent lack that resides in the right, which was so removed from the cultural process because it had *self-removed*, abdicated its responsibility to be a steward of the culture, handed over the entire means of representing the United States abroad and teaching Americans about America at home to the hard left.

But I also knew that the left's control was a false architecture born of smoke and mirrors, born of a media age in which the left controlled who was cool and who was not, who was in the in crowd and who was in the out crowd, punishing those who would step out of line and rewarding those who went with the flow. Even big stars were punished—how much more so would makeup artists doing Susan Sarandon's eyeliner be punished if they openly traded views on the war in Iraq? Leftists without credentials made it in Hollywood because they were leftists—all they had to do was show up to Jeffrey Katzenberg–sponsored fund-raisers, and Katzenberg would scratch their back. But underneath the surface, there were a lot of people who didn't agree with Katzenberg and who were waiting to be unshackled from the ideological slave ship.

Which led me to my next mission: finding as many people as I could who were right of center in Hollywood, and putting them in touch with one another, building an underground social network. It became an obsession—one that powerful people in the industry started to lead.

I started creating a Rolodex, going out to lunch with the secret Hollywood conservatives, putting them in contact with each other. People who you would never believe in a million years are con-servative, who create a left-of-center image to get work, but who despise what they have to do to get a job and long for the day true ideological freedom comes to Hollywood.

Even the left has convinced itself that these people don't exist. But they do exist, and there are huge numbers of them. Thousands of them, in every nook and cranny of the industry. You see them on-screen. You see them in the credits. You see them everywhere from the grips and the cam-eramen to the biggest directors and stars in town. And if they are introduced to each other, they will begin to break the stranglehold the left has on Hol-lywood.

I was helping introduce them, helping them make connections.

That was the first step.

The next step was exposing the left for what it truly was. That couldn't be done by simply pointing them out. It had to be done with their consent, with their input. It required a near-magic confluence of events in order to happen.

And it happened.

At the exact moment in my life when I was rec-ognizing the strength of my antileftism, my anti-communism . . . at the exact point when I was seeing that my emotions and theories were unintentionally driving me toward an accidental "culture-warrior" status…at the exact juncture when I was realizing that the most brutal, evil force I could imagine wasn't Al Qaeda or radical Islam (at least you know where they're coming from, the brutality of their mission and their anti-Western, anticlassical, liberal hatred), but the Complex surrounding me 24/7 in the form of attractive people making millions of dollars whose moral relativism and historical revisionism and collective cultural nihilism were putting them in the same boat as the martyrs of radical Islam rather than red-state Americans…at the exact time when I was undergoing the fundamental recognition that my neighbors in West Los Angeles were acting to undermine national cohesion in a time of war, which put me in a perennial state of psychic dissonance…at exactly that point, I got a phone call from Arianna Huffington.

"Do you have any ideas for a website?" she asked.

Now, by this point in our tale, Arianna Huffington had shifted her political viewpoint and was in league with the very people I had grown to oppose. How that happened is surely another story. But when that group of people came to me with Arianna as their spearhead, I saw that it was a unique and dangerous opportunity.

I approached my peers on the right with my idea, and they loved it. The idea was simple: "What," I said, "if we can get the collective left that we have dinner with, cocktail parties with, the left that talks crazy in private but only expresses itself at the Daily Kos under pseudonyms—what if we can get them all to put their names next to their crazy ideas? What if we can make it a one-stop shop for exposing liberals for who they are, and forcing them to stand by their positions?"

I presented the idea to Arianna from a different standpoint, of course. I told her she should set up a salon for like-minded thinkers to express their views. And Arianna loved it, too.

I went in with dual purposes. While the Huffington Post in theory served Arianna's and the left's goals of creating a battlefront where they could fight their battles, it served my ulterior purpose of creating preparation for talk radio and cable news, where everyone could see what lunacies constituted the thought processes of the richest noblesse oblige liberals in our land, the people who benefit the most from our way of life and yet craft the culture of our land in opposition to that way of life. Frankly, I wanted to put them on display. And, for different reasons, so did Arianna.

I knew going in that this was going to be a difficult psychological test of my resolve. After going through it, I know why CIA agents take rigorous tests in order to ascertain whether they can go through the stress of becoming a double agent, and I realized very soon thereafter that I didn't have what it took to attempt to be in consistent engagement with people whose ideas I found anathema.

Nonetheless, from November 2004 through June 1, 2005, I danced with these people, conspired with these people, and helped launch the Huffington Post. By April, however, when I realized that I wasn't going to be a spy but their manservant—I realized I couldn't live with myself or with my true friends, who relied on me to be their go-to guy for battles against the left. So I bailed out.

But it worked. I knew it had worked by the end of the launch date, May 9, 2005. I was driving down Lincoln Boulevard and listening to Michael Medved laugh aloud as he read Rob Reiner's launch-day piece, entitled "Where Have You Gone, Woodward & Bernstein?" It was a typical leftie ode to the idiotic theme that journalists are right wing, which is as stupid a belief as you're likely to find this side of John Cusack. "The so-called fourth estate is now little more than the public relations arm of a government propaganda machine in which all three branches are controlled by the same political party," Reiner wrote. "Who is watching the store?"[19]

Medved was chortling as he read this nonsense. And I felt mischievously enthralled that my mission was somewhat completed, because I had always looked at the Medveds of the world as some of the smartest people on the right—and if he got what my intention was, then I had done something very right.

The Huffington Post was great for another reason, too: the creation of Greg Gutfeld. Greg was allowed in by the Huffington Post editors as a token right-winger, and he was attacking the left from within with the most clever, insidious tactics ever. He was Jon Stewart–ing them, Stephen Colbert–ing them, and they hadn't even caught on. He made them crazy, challenged them, teased them, and confused the hell out of them. While writing for the HuffPo, Greg was consistently the biggest driver to the site, bar none. Yet he was also the writer most out of sync with the site's audience — that's how talented he is. Of course, Greg now hosts *Red Eye* on Fox News.

Perhaps the best thing about the Huffington Post, though, is something I didn't take into consideration at the time. The greatest victory for the right with regard to the site is that for years, conservatives argued that the *New York Times*, the most important journalistic entity in the United States, was radically left of center. And for years, the left denied it. But the Huffington Post was different—it was openly and loudly and radically leftist. When you read the Huffington Post, you knew there was a collective mind-set, a groupthink. And the great irony was that if you looked at the front page of the Huffington Post on any given day and matched it with the front page of the *New York Times*, they were virtually identical. If you tested the philosophical DNA of the Huffington Post and the philosophical DNA of the *New York Times*, it was obvious to anyone that they were identical twins. They were fighting the same battles, and the bylines at both places were of people who went to the same schools, married the same kind of people, voted the same way.

They were all part of the same incestuous, elitist orgy. They were all part of the power structure of Hollywood, Washington, and New York. They were all from the same group of people who made tons of money, vacationed in the nicest places, flew first class—or private, and then dictated to the rest of America how to live "sustainable" lives. It didn't matter how big Thomas Friedman's house was or Al Gore's vacation home was—they all felt the need to lecture Americans on how to behave sexually, what to eat, how to fly, where to shop...and what's more, they agreed on the answers to all of those questions.

By exposing part of the Complex via the Huffington Post, I had helped expose a major chunk of the Complex.

But I still didn't know where the Democrat-Media Complex itself had come from. It gnawed at me. Why in the world had the greatest country in history submitted itself to the evils of the Democrat-Media Complex?

Just how the hell had these nutty people gotten so much power?

CHAPTER 6

Breakthrough

Ever since college, I had experienced flashes of the Democrat-Media Complex. Then I saw it unmasked. But I didn't know exactly where that Democrat-Media Complex had been formed and why it had taken hold.

After all, I spent most of my life in a world where the Soviet Union had been destroyed. When the Berlin Wall fell in 1989, we felt that we had finally defeated global Marxism. Ronald Reagan and the United States had taken down the single largest repository of communism on the planet, and we'd done it without firing a direct shot. The whole world could see that communism didn't work—its failure was on display for the entire globe to look at and say, *So much for that.*

At least that was what we thought.

When you look at the history of the Soviet Union, what you see is the conversion of hundreds of millions to a corrupt and insidious worldview via the overpowering propaganda of communism. Yes, they used force. But they also used every means at their disposal to control the culture, the everyday lives, the very *thoughts* of their citizens.

When I was at Tulane, I saw the same cultural forces at work: the forces of the thought police, of the cultural fascisti. People in positions of power who decided what was okay to think and what to write, what words meant and who was allowed to say them. Tribunals without oversight, kids thrown out of college for uttering the wrong sentiments. Looking back, I thank God every day that I partied to excess at Tulane, because it kept me from buying into that worldview, from learning that language. If I hadn't been busy having fun, I could have become a professor, gotten tenure, and taught that cultural Marxism, propagated it for a living. I could have reinforced and propagated the Complex because it would have reinforced my position.

Later, I saw that the cultural Marxism of Tulane wasn't restricted to Tulane—it was everywhere, from the mainstream media to Hollywood to the educational system to the government. And when I began researching the origins of that pervasive cultural Marxism, I realized that this wasn't a result of

America's suddenly and spontaneously embracing a rebellious counterculture in the 1960s—it started long before that.

It started from the beginning.

The Founders of our country were realistic men who understood human nature, who recognized that people weren't infinitely changeable, that they had certain traits born into them. In *The Federalist* #51, James Madison famously said that men were not angels—that they were ambitious but rational, and that we therefore needed to construct a system of government that pitted ambition against ambition. John Adams knew government had to be limited, since "it is weakness rather than wickedness which renders men unfit to be trusted with unlimited power." Thomas Jefferson agreed.

The Founders understood human nature because they were part of the great Western tradition of philosophy and literature and history. They valued their heritage, because it sprang from basic knowledge about what human beings are. That was why the Founders were so ardent about instilling in future generations moral teaching, virtuous teaching—men were not naturally good and needed moral education.

Adam Smith's capitalism, of course, was based on the same principles, not the pure greed and selfishness Michael Moore or Barack Obama would have us believe. Smith knew that capitalism—the exchange of the products of one's best efforts for the products of someone else's best efforts—required people to act with virtue.

To sum up, the Founders' view was this: human nature is variable and requires training in virtue; no government should be given too much power, or the people comprising that government will use the power in the worst ways possible; individual freedom, when used within the boundaries of morality, is the highest good. The Constitution was written as a living testimony to this view.

The Founders' realistic view of human nature and call for limited government and individual liberty found its opponent in the philosophy of Jean-Jacques Rousseau and, later, Karl Marx. Rousseau thought that people were naturally good and were corrupted only by the development of the surrounding society (he himself was not naturally good, fathering five children out of wedlock and abandoning them all to orphanages). He also thought that modern society, created as it was to protect property rights and life, had destroyed the natural communism that prevailed before the advent of society.

To people like Rousseau, the solution to the evils of the current society was the creation of a new "social contract," one based on the "general will." The "general will" didn't need any checks and balances, because it embodied the entire will of the people. And if individuals argued with the general will, they lost.

Karl Marx's ideas picked up where Rousseau's left off. Unlike the Founders or even Rousseau, he didn't care much about human nature—for him, human nature didn't really exist. In fact, he went further: human nature was produced by surrounding society. If human nature was to be changed, it could be changed only by destroying the surrounding society.

Georg Wilhelm Friedrich Hegel provided the "dialectic theory" that backed Marx's utopianism. He believed that conflicts made the world a better place—that, basically, might made right. The struggle between two opposing ideological or philosophical forces—thesis and antithesis—would eventually end in a "synthesis" of the two sides, and that "synthesis" would be better than what had come before. Sort of like a guy (thesis) having a fight with his wife (antithesis) and then their having great makeup sex, and the product being a baby (synthesis). Only sometimes, thesis would rape antithesis in order to get to synthesis, or vice versa.

Marx married his own philosophy to Hegel in something vague and confusing called "dialectic materialism." The idea was basically that capitalism carried the seeds of its own destruction—capitalism (thesis) would be faced with the wealth gap that capitalism creates (antithesis), and that wealth gap would be solved by socialism/communism (synthesis).

This is what Marx meant in his famous statement in *The Communist Manifesto*: "The history of all hitherto existing society is the history of class struggles." In the final conflict, the workers would win and a communist synthesis would be established. Happy day!

This all sounds confusing and would make anyone with common sense stop and say, "Wait a minute—explain that one slowly, and tell me why it isn't intellectual babble." Unfortunately, there's only one problem: important people in America believed it.

Let me continue with this brief history lesson.

President Teddy Roosevelt is on Mount Rushmore. Even though Teddy was a Republican, he was no conservative—he was a "Progressive." Progressivism was a strain in American thought that merged the Hegelian dialectic with Marxism, backed by a rosy Rousseau-ian view of humanity and the general will—basically, it was soft Marxism without the class struggle.

There was only one problem, of course—here in

America, we have something they didn't have in Germany or even Britain: a Constitution that protects individual liberty. But that didn't stop Teddy. Progressivism, you see, was active. And that was the thing about Teddy—he always had to keep himself busy and powerful. Like an early-twentieth-century Barack Obama, Teddy slammed those who disagreed with him, characterizing typical American self-reliance as selfishness. Collectivism was the new cool.

Those who stand for Progressivism, said Teddy, "stand for the forward movement...for the uplift and betterment, who have faith in the people." Ends, not means, matter: "We of today who stand for the Progressive movement here in the United States are not wedded to any particular kind of machinery, save solely as means to the end desired. Our aim is to secure the real and not the nominal rule of the people."[1] That's scary stuff—the business of government is all about means, which is why the Constitution is mostly a document describing how things get done, not what things should get done. Once a president starts ignoring means to get to ends, we've got a serious constitutional problem on our hands.

Teddy was a serious constitutional problem. His Progressivism had practical consequences. In his 1910 speech "The New Nationalism," he compared wealth inequalities with the Civil War and said that individual rights had to take a backseat to the common interest.[2]

In that same speech, Teddy went over the Niagara Falls of Progressive ideology in a wooden barrel—he actually said that people couldn't be permitted to make money unless it was of benefit to the community for them to do so. "We grudge no man a fortune in civil life if it is honorably obtained and well used. It is not even enough that it should have been gained without doing damage to the community. We should permit it to be gained only so long as the gaining represents benefit to the community," he said. This was Marx in action. With a president behind Marx, his ideals were now competing on equal footing with the founding fathers'.

Teddy's Progressivism had its most dramatic effects in shaping a new view of the Constitution. He summed up his thoughts about the Constitution in one line: "To hell with the Constitution when the people want coal!"[3]

Teddy's ideological heir didn't make it to the White House until 1912. His name was Woodrow Wilson.

Wilson was the proto-egghead, a political science professor and Princeton dean who frowned upon democracy. Our American egalitarianism was beginning to be replaced by elites who knew better than the masses. Wilson had imbibed the best of European philosophy (namely, Hegel and his heirs) while studying at Johns Hopkins University, which was the first American university to mirror the German university model. Unsurprisingly, he rejected the idea of government by the people, and he rejected the old-fashioned notion that founding principles of free enterprise and private property should be protected by checks and balances on the growth of government. Government, he said, was a living thing, and it needed the freedom to do its magical work. Because government had stuff to do, the Constitution was a waste of time for Wilson. It held the people back. "Justly revered as our great constitution is, it could be stripped off and thrown aside like a garment, and the nation would still stand forth clothed in the living vestment of flesh and sinew, warm with the heart-blood of one people, ready to recreate constitutions and laws."[4]

Mostly, the Constitution was standing in the way of the grand Hegelian synthesis of government power in the name of socialism. Wilson felt that true democracy and socialism were not just compatible—they were indistinguishable. All individual rights were subject to the rights of the state: *"Men as communities are supreme over men as individuals."*[5]

Both Roosevelt and Wilson were far less concerned about the rights of individuals or the value of republicanism; it was the job of Great Leaders to hand down good governance. They thought that great decisions should be made on high by men of high thought, and that the dirty process of democracy just blocked any chance at true change. This philosophy paved the way for FDR, and it echoes all the way down to Obama.

Fortunately for America, after World War I, Wilson was extremely unpopular, and Wilson's exit led off a decade of constitutional retrenchment.

But in Europe, dirty business was afoot.

Despite the fact that Marxism made headway in terms of policy in the United States and other Western European countries in the early part of the twentieth century, orthodox Marxists had a major problem by the end of the 1910s: the actual worldwide Marxist revolution really hadn't ignited. Not only hadn't it happened, workers had spent the better part of five years murdering each other en masse in World War I. Marx's dialectical prophecy had been proved false.

But just because Marx's dialectic materialism had been proved false, and just because soon the new Soviet Union would be slaughtering its own citizens at record rates, didn't mean that the Marxist intellectuals were going to give up on worldwide revolution.

That was where Antonio Gramsci and Gyorgy Lukacs came in.

Gramsci was an Italian socialist who saw tearing down society as the necessary precondition for the eventual victory of global Marxism. Marxism simply hadn't won because men were weak. And men were weak because they were the products of a capitalist society. "Man is above all else mind, consciousness," Gramsci wrote in 1916. "That is, he is a product of history, not of nature. There is no other way of explaining why socialism has not come into existence already."[6]

Lukacs built on Gramsci, deciding that Marx's dialectic materialism wasn't really a prophetic tool for predicting the future—it was a tool for tearing down society itself. Simply destroying the status quo in the minds of the people would bring Marxism.

Lukacs's view was so influential that for a time, he actually became deputy commissar of culture in Hungary, where he proceeded to push a radical sex-ed program encouraging free love and rejection of Judeo-Christian morality. In that role, he tried to live out his ideology of destruction: "I saw the revolutionary destruction of society as the one and only solution.... A worldwide overturning of values cannot take place without the annihilation of the old values and the creation of new ones by the revolutionaries."[7] Fortunately, the people of Hungary weren't nuts, so they dumped him.

That left Lukacs unemployed. But not for long.

Felix Weil was a young radical from Frankfurt, Germany, and a devotee of Marx. He, like Lukacs, saw the problems of implementing socialism—namely, that nobody really liked it very much. But like most of today's leftie college students who live off their parents' money while preaching the downfall of the capitalist system, he was rich. So he used his granddaddy's money to fund the Institute for Social Research, which was really a precursor to John Podesta's "Center for American Progress"—funded by Hungarian-born George Soros.

To staff this new institute, which quickly became known as the Frankfurt School, Weil brought in, along with Lukacs, a Marxist philosopher named Max Horkheimer. Lukacs didn't last long, but Horkheimer did. At the Frankfurt School, he coined a term that would embody the whole corrupt philosophy of his fellow travelers' mission to destroy society and culture using the Marxist dialectic: critical theory.

Critical theory was exactly the material we were taught at Tulane. It was, quite literally, a theory of criticizing everyone and everything everywhere.

It was an attempt to tear down the social fabric by using all the social sciences (sociology, psychology, economics, political science, etc.); it was an infinite and unending criticism of the status quo, adolescent rebellion against all established social rules and norms.

Critical theory, says Horkheimer, is "suspicious of the very categories of better, useful, appropriate, productive, and valuable, as those are understood in the present order."[8] So if you liked ice cream better than cake, or thought a hammer might be more useful than a screwdriver in a particular situation, you were speaking on behalf of the status quo. The real idea behind all of this was to make society totally unworkable by making everything basically meaningless. Critical theory does not create; it only destroys, as Horkheimer himself openly stated, "Above all...critical theory has no material accomplishments to show for itself."[9] No wonder my thought upon graduating was that getting a job was selling out.

When Horkheimer took over the institute in 1930, he filled it up with fellow devotees of critical theory like Theodor Adorno, Erich Fromm, and Herbert Marcuse. Each agreed with the central idea of critical theory, namely that all of society had to be criticized ad nauseam, all social institutions leveled, all traditional concepts decimated. Marcuse later summed it up well: "One can rightfully speak of a cultural revolution, since the protest is directed toward the whole cultural establishment, including the morality of existing society.... What we must undertake is a type of diffuse and dispersed disintegration of the system."[10]

Again, where am I going with all of this philosophical jabberwocky? Well, all of these boring and bleating philosophers might have faded into oblivion as so many Marxist theorists have, but the rise of Adolf Hitler prevented that. With Hitler's rise, they had to flee (virtually all of them—Horkheimer, Marcuse, Adorno, Fromm—were of Jewish descent). And they had no place to go.

Except the United States.

The United States' tradition of freedom and liberty, its openness to outside ideas, and our highest value, freedom of speech, ended up making all America vulnerable to those who would exploit those ideals. We welcomed the Frankfurt School. We accepted them with open arms. They took full advantage. They walked right into our cultural institutions, and as they started to put in place their leadership, their language, and their lexicon, too many chose to ignore them. And the most dangerous thing you can do with a driven leftist intellectual clique is to ignore it.

We always feel that our incredible traditions of freedom and liberty will convert those who show up on our shores, that they will appreciate the way of life we have created—isn't that why they wanted to come here in the first place? We can't imagine anyone coming here, experiencing the true wonder that is living in this country, and wanting to destroy that. But that's exactly what the Frankfurt School wanted to do.

These were not happy people looking for a new lease on life. When they moved to California, they simply couldn't deal with the change of scenery—there was cognitive dissonance. Horkheimer and Adorno and depressive allies like Bertolt Brecht moved into a house in Santa Monica on Twenty-sixth Street, coincidentally, the epicenter of my childhood. They had moved to heaven on earth from Nazi Germany and apparently could not handle the fun, the sun, and the roaring good times. Ingratitude is not strong enough a word to describe these hideous malcontents.

If only they had had IKEA furniture, this would have made for a fantastic season of *The Real World*.

Brecht and his ilk were the Kurt Cobains of their day: massively depressed, nihilistic people who wore full suits in eighty-degree weather while living in a house by the beach. As Adam Cohen wrote in the *New York Times,* these were "dyspeptic critics of American culture. Several landed in Southern California where they were disturbed by the consumer culture and the gospel of relentless cheeriness. Depressive by nature, they focused on the disappointments and venality that surrounded them and how unnecessary it all was. It could be paradise, Theodor Adorno complained, but it was only California."[11]

Adorno was wrong. It was paradise. To the rest of the world, America's vision was a vision of paradise. And these Marxists were here to try to destroy the best lifestyle man had ever created.

If I could go back in a time machine, I would go back to kick these malcontents in their shins.

Members of the Frankfurt School had some American allies—men who had accepted the Roosevelt/ Wilson synthesis of Hegel and Marx, and who were now looking for the next step. The Frankfurt School had been sending mailers out to prominent fellow-traveler sociologists in the United States for some years and creating connections with them.

Meanwhile, Columbia University's Sociology department was dying. They needed new blood, and they liked what they saw in the Frankfurt School.

All the Frankfurt School had to do was to get into the country, and they'd take their place in the hallowed halls of American academia. Fortunately for them, there was an organization called the Institute of International Education, specifically devoted to helping fleeing scholars from Germany. The man who held the post of assistant secretary of the Emergency Committee in Aid of Displaced Foreign Scholars was one Edward R. Murrow, who helped ship in many of the Frankfurt School's greatest minds. Later, Senator Joe McCarthy would try to pillory Murrow in revenge for Murrow's coverage of the McCarthy hearings by citing Murrow's involvement with the Institute of International Education, but by then McCarthy was finished.

In any case, once in the country, the Frankfurt School was almost immediately accepted at Columbia University. It was a marriage made in hell.

With their tentacles affixed to the institutions of American higher education, the Frankfurt School philosophy began eking its way into every crevice of American culture. Horkheimer's "critical theory" became a staple of Philosophy, History, and English courses across the country. Horkheimer himself took his show on the road, from Columbia to Los Angeles to the University of Chicago.

Meanwhile, Erich Fromm, one of the Frankfurt School's main thinkers, was pushing cultural Marxism through psychology by blaming Western tradition for the rise of Nazism and the rejection of Marxism.[12]

This was a fiction, of course, convenient rewriting of science to meet a political agenda. Marxism is just as totalitarian as Nazism, so it would make sense that those who love communism quickly fell in love with Nazism in Germany, and those who resisted communism would resist Nazism. But Fromm had a convenient answer to protect the Marxists: Marxists had not gone Nazi; resisters to Marxism had gone Nazi! How did Fromm know this? Because those who submit to Marxism love freedom, while those who fight Marxism are secretly repressed. Soldiers are authoritarian because they take orders. Small businessmen are authoritarian in their unconscious desire to submit to "economic laws."[13] Leftists today still call their opponents Nazis on the basis of this flawed and inane psychoanalysis.

Early on, Fromm embraced the ideas of Frankfurt School fellow Wilhelm Reich, who felt that psychological problems largely stemmed from sexual repression, and said that sexual liberation from societal mores could cure large numbers of people. Reich (whose psychoanalysis included disrobing his patients and then touching them) helped place the foundations of modern feminism, arguing that "the repression of the sexual needs creates a general weakening of intellect and emotional functioning; in particular, it makes people lack independence, will-power and critical faculties." Marriage, he wrote, ruins lives: "Marital misery, to the extent to which it does not exhaust itself in the marital conflicts, is poured out over the children."[14]

Fromm also expanded on the parenting ideas of Lukacs and John Dewey, who rejected parental authority, telling parents to stand by and let their children reinvent the wheel through experience. Fromm's philosophy was imbibed by a young socialist student named Benjamin Spock, who would go on to shape a generation of parents with his child-rearing book *The Common Sense Book of Baby and Child Care*, which helped launch the self-esteem movement.[15]

At the same time, Frankfurt School scholar Theodor Adorno was sliding Marxism into the American consciousness by attacking popular trends in the world of art. First teaching at Columbia and then later at Princeton, he argued that television and movies were problematic because they appealed to the masses—but television and the movies weren't catering to the public tastes, they were shaping them, Adorno argued. Popular art and culture had destroyed true art, which is always used for revolutionary purposes, he said.[16] All popular art therefore had to be criticized as a symptom of the capitalist system. All art had to be torn down. Performance art and modern art found their philosophical foundation in Adorno. The long line stretching from *Piss Christ* to Karen Finley smearing herself with feces to Susan Sarandon celebrating being hit with transsexual projectile vomit all had its roots with Adorno.

This nihilistic influence in art, reinforcing the destruction of cultural norms, means that many grown adults have never experienced an epoch in which the transcendent and the innately beautiful have been celebrated as the artistic ideal. And it all started because a Rat Pack of Nazi-fleeing depressives couldn't appreciate leaving the world's most oppressive place for the world's most spectacularly free and beautiful place.

Santa Monica. Google it. It takes a sincerely deranged soul to want to deconstruct the good life and the optimistic citizenry in order to create mass intellectual and spiritual misery. But that's exactly what they did. And as they constructed their philosophical dystopia, all the pieces of the modern leftist puzzle began falling into place.

But all of these major contributors to the Frankfurt School of thought paled in comparison to Herbert Marcuse, the founder of the "New Left." Marcuse was a former student of future Nazi philo-

sopher Martin Heidegger, the father of "deconstruction," a process by which every thought or
writing from the past had to be examined and torn
down as an outgrowth of its social milieu. Heidegger wasn't shy about his intentions; he longed for
the moment "when the spiritual strength of the
West fails and its joints crack, when the moribund
semblance of culture caves in and drags all forces
into confusion and lets them suffocate in mad-
ness."[17]

Marcuse joined the Frankfurt School in 1933
and quickly became a leader of the movement.
After he moved to the United States and became
a citizen, he was hired by FDR's Office of War
Information to create anti-Nazi propaganda, despite his Marxism. He also worked in the Office
of Strategic Services (the pre-CIA OSS), and the
State Department, where he worked to prevent the
United States from pushing Germany away from
democratic socialism. He taught at Columbia,
then Harvard, then Brandeis, and then finally at the
University of California in San Diego.

He really hit his stride in 1955, however, with
the publication of *Eros and Civilization*. The book
essentially made Wilhelm Reich's case that sexual
liberation was the best counter to the psychological
ills of society. Marcuse preferred a society of "poly-
morphous perversity,"[18] which is just what it

sounds like—people having sex every which way, with whatever.

It wasn't so much the freshness of Marcuse's message that made the difference (it wasn't a fresh message) as his timing—the kids brought up with Fromm and Freud and Spock were coming of age. The misplaced guilt of the Greatest Generation brought forth a new generation free to embrace Marcuse. While similar philosophies of sex had failed in the 1920s, 1930s, and 1940s, by the 1950s the men and women who had suffered through the Great Depression and fought in World War II were determined to raise privileged kids who would never have to actually fight for their country or work for their food. The result was a group of kids ready and able to participate in the sexual revolution promised by the Frankfurt School. Marcuse excused sexual promiscuity as the fulfillment of the need for the people to rise up against Western civilization and to free themselves of the sexual repression it created. Not a hard sell for teenagers.

It was no wonder that in a very real sense, his followers believed they were doing something special when they made love, not war (a slogan attributed to Marcuse himself)—they were using their sexual energy to bind the world together rather than destroy it, as sexual repression would do. While Marcuse may not have been the most important intellectual force behind the Frankfurt School, he was its most devious and effective marketer. The advertising adage "Sex sells" was applied to selling a generation on the idea that their parents' values and ideals were repressive and evil. (Where geographically did Marcuse come to this nihilistic understanding? The picturesque cliffs of La Jolla, overlooking the Pacific Ocean.)

Marcuse carried his "critical theory" in another destructive direction as well: while repeating the Marxist trope that the workers of the world would eventually unite—he saw the third world's "anti-colonial" movements as evidence that Marx was right—he recognized that in the United States there would be no such uprising by the working class. He therefore needed a different set of interest groups to tear down capitalism using his critical theory. And he found those groups in the racial, ethnic, and sexual groups that hated the old order. These victimized interest groups rightly opposed all the beauties of Western civilization "with all the defiance, and the hatred, and the joy of rebellious victims, defining their own humanity against the definitions of the masters."[19]

Marcuse's mission was to dismantle American society by using diversity and "multiculturalism" as crowbars with which to pry the structure apart, piece by piece. He wanted to set blacks in opposition to whites, set all "victim groups" in opposition to the society at large. Marcuse's theory of victim groups as the new proletariat, combined with Horkheimer's critical theory, found an outlet in academia, where it became the basis for the post-structural movement—Gender Studies, LGBT/ "Queer" Studies, African-American Studies, Chicano Studies, etc. All of these "Blank Studies" brazenly describe their mission as tearing down traditional Judeo-Christian values and the accepted traditions of Western culture, and placing in their stead a moral relativism that equates all cultures and all philosophies—except for Western civilization, culture, and philosophy, which are "exploitative" and "bad."

Marcuse was widely accepted in the 1960s by the student movement—so much so that students in Paris during the 1968 uprising marched with banners reading "Marx, Mao, and Marcuse."

But he still wasn't winning in America. Marcuse had a big, big problem: America's founding ideology is still far sexier than that of the Marxists, who insist on a tyrannical state of equality rather than freedom with personal responsibility. Even if Marcuse was promising unending sex, drugs, and rock and roll, most Americans were more interested in living in liberty with their families, in a society that values virtue and hard work rather than promiscuity and decadence.

So Marcuse had to find a way to defy the opposition. He found it in what he termed "repressive tolerance." In 1965, Marcuse wrote an essay by that name in which he argued that tolerance was good only if nondominating ideas were allowed to flourish—and that nondominating ideas could flourish only if dominating ideas were shut down. "[T]he realization of the objective of tolerance," he wrote, "would call for intolerance toward prevailing policies, attitudes, opinions, and the extension of tolerance to policies, attitudes, and opinions which are outlawed or suppressed." America was experiencing a "repressive tolerance" under which dissenting viewpoints were stifled; what it needed was "partisan tolerance."[20]

In other words, if you disagreed with Marcuse, you should be forcefully shut up, according to Marcuse. This made political debate very convenient for him and his allies. This totalitarianism is now standard practice on college campuses, in the media, and in Hollywood—the very places that the Frankfurt School sought to control.

The First Amendment—the same instrument that allowed the Frankfurt School to land on our shores and express their pernicious ideas in freedom—was now curtailed by those who had benefitted from it. Marcuse called for a tyranny of the minority, since the tyranny of the majority could not be overcome without a total shutdown.

There's another name for Marcuse's "partisan tolerance": Political Correctness.

In fact, the term *"political correctness"* came from one of Marcuse's buddies: Mao Tse-tung. Mao used the term to differentiate between those who had "scientifically correct" views and those who did not; those who did were termed "politically correct." In 1963, just two years before Marcuse's "repressive tolerance," Mao came out with an essay entitled "Where Do Correct Ideas Come From?"[21] In that essay, he argued that the Marxist society determines correct ideas, and all incorrect ideas must be put out of their misery. Mao thought it. Marcuse thought it. And his ideological heirs thought it and still think it. Hello, neighbor!

And so Marxism came stealthily to our shores, squatted here, planted its roots, and grew like a weed—all before we even noticed it. It happened at the university level and at the governmental level and at the media level. We didn't notice because we couldn't read the rhetorical garbage these jokers were spewing, and we didn't think it was important—"Our Constitution survived a revolution and a Civil War and two World Wars. Why should we worry about a few German eggheads?" Especially since America was economically thriving under such "oppression."

The foundations of the Complex had been built. But we still couldn't see the Complex itself—the Complex was hidden under paragraphs of obscure text and in college curricula at places like Tulane University, under the unlikely auspices of "American Studies." Talk about a wolf in sheep's clothing. It all seemed so benign, and we figured that if college students went off and had sex and did drugs and engaged in teenage rebellious decadence, oh well, they'd eventually come back to the Constitution, just the way their parents had.

We slept while the other side armed, and while we snoozed they secretly stole away our defensive weaponry—our allegiance to the Constitution and to freedom of speech and opinion.

It was only when they fired the first shots over our bow that we noticed we were unarmed, and that they had weaponized the cloudy bacteria of their philosophy into full-bore ideological anthrax, ready to deploy on a moment's notice.

The line was becoming clear. Marx and Hegel had paved the way for the Progressives, who in turn had paved the way for the Frankfurt School, who had then attacked the American way of life by pushing "cultural Marxism" through "critical theory." The Frankfurt School thinkers had come up with the rationale for radical environmentalism, artistic communism, psychological deconstruction of their opponents, and multiculturalism. Most of all, they had come up with the concept of "repressive tolerance," aka political correctness.

They had penetrated the academies—my American Studies program at Tulane had far more Adorno and Gramsci and Horkheimer and Marcuse than Twain or Jefferson or Lincoln. There was some trickle-down intellectualism going on— all the college students who worked through these programs and took swigs from the Frankfurt School bottle labeled "Drink Me" shrank mentally and ended up as parts of the Complex. But that didn't explain how American society as a whole was taken over by this stuff. I just couldn't understand it: how did Frankfurt School philosophy, which is obviously complicated, highfalutin stuff, become a mass psychosis? How did it trick so many millions of people?

And I had another question, too. Frankfurt School philosophy was all about criticizing from the outside. It was about tearing down society by taking it apart, piece by piece, razing it to the ground. That stuff doesn't go over very well in this country, because people here are generally happy—we don't see Disneyland as an emblem of corporate greed or capitalistic exploitation, we see it as a fun place to take our kids, and if somebody tried to tear down Disneyland in the name of the collective, we'd have a shit fit. So how did this outsiders' philosophy penetrate our hearts and our minds? How did the Complex, which was a huge philosophical system designed to take America head-on, recede into the background so much that a few decades later, we can't even recognize that it exists?

Then I read Saul Alinsky's *Rules for Radicals*: if Marcuse was the Jesus of the New Left, then Alinsky was his Saint Paul, proselytizing and dumbing down Marcuse's message, making it practical, and convincing leaders to make it the official religion of the United States, even if that meant discarding the old secular religion of the United States, the Constitution.

Rules for Radicals might just as well be entitled *How to Take Over America from the Inside*. It's theory made flesh. Alinsky laid it out step-by-step, but we were too busy fighting the results to read his game plan.

Let's start by noting who Saul Alinsky was. Alinsky was an avowed communist dedicated to installing communism in America from the inside, using the most clever tactical means he could devise. He was born in 1909 in Chicago, and like his Frankfurt School counterparts, he quickly migrated toward Marx. He attended the University of Chicago and majored in Archaeology, but dumped that after he couldn't get a job. After working as a criminologist, he became a community organizer—yes, a community organizer—for the Congress of Industrial Organizations (CIO), a major union run by John L. Lewis, an anticommunist leftist who actually pushed for the election of Republican Wendell Willkie in the 1940 election in the hopes that if Willkie were elected with CIO help, the CIO could win major concessions. From Lewis, whom Alinsky called "one of the most outstanding figures of our time,"[22] Alinsky learned hardnosed tactics. And he applied those hardnosed tactics to his own Marxism.

One of the crucial lessons he learned was that he had to work from the inside. Whereas New Left leaders like Marcuse preferred to bash the system from the outside and alienate all those who were part of it, Alinsky knew that it was more important to pose as an insider to achieve his aims.

It worked brilliantly. *Time* magazine bought into Alinsky's act in a 1970 profile: "It is not too much to argue that American democracy is being altered by Alinsky's ideas. In an age of dissolving political labels, he is a radical—but not in the usual sense, and he is certainly a long way removed from New Left extremists." This, of course, was not true—not in the slightest. His own beliefs were intensely close to those of Marcuse and the Frankfurt School— it was only his practicality and pragmatism that distinguished him and made him infinitely more effective.

Alinsky took on the trappings of American constitutionalism in order to insinuate himself insidiously into the American consciousness. He scorned flag-burning as counterproductive. He talked about the Founders on a regular basis. He even posed as a conservative when it suited his purposes. *Time* sums up the popular view of Alinsky, a view he cultivated with minute forethought: "Alinsky claims to be doing nothing more un-American than following the precepts of the Founding Fathers. In the Federalist papers, James Madison warned against allowing any class or faction to acquire too much power. In his own way, Alinsky is trying to redress the balance of power within contemporary America. If the desire to preserve basic American principles makes one a conservative, then he indeed qualifies.... He surely offers proof—if any is needed—that significant change can be accomplished within the American system."[23] This about a man who constantly cited communism as his governing philosophy! It is no wonder Alinsky was so effective.

Alinsky summarized his strategy for instituting Marxist change in his 1971 book, *Rules for Radicals: A Pragmatic Primer for Realistic Radicals*. It's actually an excellent book, clear where Marcuse is foggy, irreverent where Adorno is stagnant, dirty and funny where Horkheimer is abstruse and boring.

The book's dedication page explains in a nutshell what was so dangerous about Alinsky—he mixed a dash of religious fervor, a sprinkle of American founding talk, and a heavy dose of "kiss my ass" into a concoction that was relatively easy and fun to swallow. The first page has an epigraph from Rabbi Hillel, one from Thomas Paine, and finally, Alinsky's "kiss my ass" epigraph: "Lest we forget at least an over-the-shoulder acknowledgment to the very first radical: from all our legends, mythology, and history (and who is to know where mythology leaves off and history begins—or which is which), the very first radical known to man who rebelled against the establishment and did it so effectively that he at least won his own kingdom—Lucifer."[24] Only a true egoist would cite himself in his epigraph, but that was what made Alinsky so unique—his brazen disregard for tradition, sewn together with the dressings of majority society.

Alinsky immediately makes clear where he stands on politics: he's a Marxist, and a pragmatic Marxist at that. Alinsky's role, as a pragmatic communist, is to succeed where his "fellow radicals" had failed. He despises those impractical Marxists who "panic and run, rationalizing that the system is going to collapse anyway of its own rot and corruption," those who go "hippie or yippie, taking drugs, trying communes, anything to escape," those who "went berserk...the Weathermen and their like." He laughs at the college students who embrace Marcuse-ian philosophy while doing nothing, those who spend their time cribbing from the communist puppetmasters and wear Che T-shirts.[25]

He also knows that America's openness provides communists the opportunity to destroy American values, which makes working from the outside a waste of time. Militant outsider-ism is counterproductive. Alinsky, first and foremost, knows that to win, communists must communicate in the language of the people. They must embrace the people, not scorn them. They must embrace the world as it is, not as they wish it were. "As an organizer," Alinsky writes in Donald Rumsfeld–like language, "I start from where the world is, as it is, not as I would like it to be.... That means working inside the system."[26]

The people, Alinsky thinks, are like happy sheep. In order to steer them in the politically correct direction, they first must be made unhappy, and that unhappiness will result in passivity, then finally in discontent, and then, in the end, revolution. Incrementalism, as Frankfurt School's Antonio Gramsci taught, is the name of the game. And the only way to begin opening the door to the revolution is to make people unhappy with the status quo. Revolutionaries aren't supposed to afflict the comfortable and comfort the afflicted—they're supposed to afflict everybody, making them long for a mass overturning of the system as a whole. After calling for the destruction of the system John Adams helped create, Alinsky, with his typical aplomb, actually quotes John Adams to back him up. (Adams must have been spinning wildly in his grave as Alinsky dug out his dog-eared Adams quote book.)

Alinsky's clever merging of fake founding philosophy with his own Marxism led him to internal contradictions that would have sunk a lesser ego. While championing "freedom," for example, he hated the idea of individual freedom the Founders loved—he wanted "communal freedom," which is to say tyranny led by the government. "The greatest enemy of individual freedom is the individual himself," he wrote.[27] This is typically Rousseau-ian messaging—community trumps the individual, and in fact, individualism can only exist within the body politic. In other words, workers of the world unite—from within the system. And he united his ideas under the rubric of "change." Yes, "change."[28] He also liked "hope," because his personal philosophy "is anchored in optimism."[29] Sound familiar?

Alinsky says he's not looking for a Marxist revolution, but he *is* looking to provide a manual for the "Have-Nots" against the "Haves."[30] That sounds an awful lot like Marxism to me.

All of this is great rhetoric, but how would Alinsky actually build his forces? How would he find his minions?

By finding the raw materials. He tells us straight out what he's looking for in a "community organizer."

First off, he looks for *flexibility*.[31] That means moving from method to method, argument to argument, fighting like a guerrilla rather than like a coordinated army. Don't worry about methodological consistency, says Alinsky—just do what you have to in order to win. Alinsky believes that the ends justify the means as a general rule. He believes that fearing corruption of your internal values only leads to paralysis, and that the only way to truly win is to abandon yourself wholly to your ends. As Stalin would have put it, you have to break a few eggs to make an omelet. Alinsky liked omelets.

This obviously runs directly counter to the notions of Judeo-Christian morality, which ardently state that right ends cannot justify wrong means. That is why American society has such a tough time handling Alinsky's acolytes: he didn't play by their rules, and they couldn't play by his rules. Alinsky simply didn't care about Judeo-Christian morality—he was a total moral relativist who declared, without batting an eye, "One man's positive is another man's negative."[32] He actually made the argument that Nazi resisters weren't objectively moral—to the Nazis. Winners write history, says Alinsky, so you'd better be the winner. That holds particularly true in war, where "the end justifies almost any means"—and Alinsky views all politics (and actually, all life) as war. If you have the option of using moral means, by all means use them, says Alinsky—if not, screw 'em. As he said in his usual colorful language, the alternative to corrupt victory is to "go home [defeated] with my ethical hymen intact."[33] And he was no virgin.

His bottom line is plain and unvarnished: Kick ass and then pretend you were doing the moral thing. Lie, cheat, and steal for victory. If you have to lie to win, then lie and win, then lie about your lie. If you have to win with brutality, then be brutal and win, and then rewrite history about your brutality. Always cloak your goals in widely agreed-upon American terms that people buy into. Things like the Declaration of Independence or the "common welfare" provision of the Constitution. Sure, you may be standing for none of those things. But that doesn't matter—victory is what matters. It's the Chicago way.

Second, Alinsky looks for *confidence*. Weak-willed people never win, and those who doubt themselves are weak-willed.[34] It takes confidence to go after your opposition with a chainsaw. Those who have self-confidence will not shy away from conflict, which is an essential feature of progress, he says (channeling Hegel).

Third, Alinsky espouses the value of *experience*. Education as a community organizer means embracing Rousseau-like experiential learning, since history doesn't repeat itself—all history is changeable and changing. This is also an excellent rationalization for young people to ignore the wisdom of the past—this time, just like every time, things are different.

Fourth, Alinsky suggests certain personal qualities in organizers. Here are some of the most important.

Sincerity: the good community organizer must

be absolutely honest and sincere. This is good advice for any politician, but it is excellent advice for someone trying to work with populations different from his/her own.

Curiosity and *irreverence*: the organizer must be curious, because everything needs to be questioned. Values must be questioned. Morals must be questioned. This is basically critical theory in practice. Alinsky's focus on irreverence is particularly important: "To the questioner nothing is sacred." Again, this is critical theory in its most basic practical form.

A sense of humor: This is probably the most important quality Alinsky mentions. Humor is a weapon to be deployed as often as possible — it is almost impossible to defend against. It is the weapon the Frankfurt School lacked — their seriousness made them boring and inaccessible. Alinsky is no such thing. He is hilarious, and that hilarity breeds the sort of social change only a Jon Stewart or a Stephen Colbert could bring about rather than a Noam Chomsky.

When it comes to humor, Alinsky has no problem going lowest common denominator, which is what makes him so effective. It's one thing to pun like Shakespeare when you're in polite company, but social change isn't effected in polite company — it's effected in the streets, with the people.

And people love base humor. In the book, Alinsky makes jokes about sex and farting, both in order to shock and to cross cultural boundaries—after all, everybody poops. Conservatives are afraid to talk in these terms, and that's one reason why they lose young people in particular.

As it stands, the Frankfurt School–taught left is fighting the political battle on both the political and the cultural battlefields. Conservatives are fighting it only on the political battlefield. That means that art, humor, song, theater, television, film, dance are all devices used every day in order to influence the hearts and minds of the American people. Conservatives have to pray that their kids will eventually discover George Will's column to knock some sense into them.

Once he's got his organizers, his soldiers for the battlefield, Alinsky lays out his tactics. He's not just Machiavelli—he's Sun Tzu. Here are his rules for tactical warfare, quoted verbatim in italics:

1. *Power is not only what you have, but what the enemy thinks you have.* Deception is useful, and giving the other side incomplete information is just as useful. If it was good enough for Gideon, it's good enough for Alinsky.

2. *Never go outside the experience of your people.* You can't preach abortion to Catholic priests or pork to Jews. Work with the material you have, or you'll confuse your own forces.

3. *Wherever possible go outside of the experience of the enemy.* If they can't handle you because they've never handled anything like you, you'll win.

4. *Make the enemy live up to their own book of rules.* Alinsky writes, "You can kill them with this, for they can no more obey their own rules than the Christian church can live up to Christianity." *Hypocrisy* is obviously the key word here, and it's the left's favorite charge for the simple reason that the vast majority of people with standards are "hypocrites" at some point in their lives.

5. *Ridicule is man's most potent weapon.* Just ask Gerald Ford (Chevy Chase), George W. Bush (Will Ferrell), or Sarah Palin (Tina Fey).

6. *A good tactic is one that your people enjoy.* You're not going to win if your people are bored out of their minds.

7. *A tactic that drags on too long becomes a drag.*

8. *Keep the pressure on.*

9. *The threat is usually more terrifying than the thing itself.* Don't be scared of the opposition — even if they level their most feared weapon at you, it probably won't be that bad. Meanwhile, level threats whenever possible, because that will scare the opposition.

10. *The major premise for tactics is the development of operations that will maintain a constant pressure upon the opposition.* Pressure causes reactions, and you can work off of the reaction of your target.

11. *If you push a negative hard and deep enough it will break through into its counterside.* Find the enemy's most cherished belief, then exploit it against your target. Alinsky uses the example of passive resistance in India — by exploiting the British pride in their civility, Gandhi defeated them. It goes without saying that the Frankfurt School used precisely this tactic in twisting their First Amendment freedoms against the First Amendment in the United States.

12. *The price of a successful attack is a constructive alternative.* Make sure you have a plan once you've achieved your goals.

13. *Pick the target, freeze it, personalize, and polarize it.* This is the most important and famous of Alinsky's rules. You have to pick a target, then freeze it and prevent it from shifting blame elsewhere, then personalize it by making sure that it is something specific and identifiable rather than general, and finally, polarize it by demonizing it. It does you no good to talk about the pros and cons of your target—you must show the target as entirely evil, and yourself as entirely good. This is commonly known as the politics of personal destruction. (See Palin, Sarah.)

Finally, Alinsky provides a simple reminder: *the real action is in the enemy's reaction.* You must provoke your enemy into reacting so that you can work off of the reaction. If you do a good enough job, you can force them to make a mistake. When they do, you must be ready to exploit it.

It's worth exploring one of Alinsky's case studies in order to see these rules in action. In 1964, he moved to Rochester, New York, in the aftermath of race riots and targeted Eastman Kodak, the largest company in town by far. He quickly implemented rules 13 (target, freeze, personalize, and polarize) and 5 (mockery is the best strategy). The media interviewed him when he stepped off the plane in Rochester, asking him what he thought of the town. "It is a huge southern plantation transplanted north," Alinsky said.

This got him the reaction he was looking for from the opposition, which gave him more targets to attack. W. Allen Wallis, president of the University of Rochester and director at Eastman Kodak, went after Alinsky. Alinsky responded by comparing Wallis to George Wallace of Alabama.[35] Did it matter if the charge was true? Of course not. But it was effective.

Putting into action the rest of his rules—using the law as a tool to make the establishment obey its own rules, moving outside the experience of the enemy, letting your soldiers enjoy the experience, etc.—Alinsky suggested another tactic in Rochester, a flamboyant and outrageous tactic sure to get a response simply because of its pure outrageousness. He suggested that blacks buy tickets to the Rochester symphony orchestra, eat beans beforehand, then fart over and over again to disturb the upper-class white folks.[36]

This is brilliant. Farting for a cause is about as smart as you can get, because there's no way to defend against it—it's not illegal to fart, it's completely offensive and makes people uncomfortable, and even as black folks are passing gas in a chamber music concert, they get to claim the moral high ground and pillory their enemies as racists.

Alinsky is infuriatingly awesome—he's smart where his compatriots are "intellectual," and always reaches his intended audience, something professors often fail to do. He knows what he wants and how to get it, and he makes it easy for anyone to follow his pattern. The trickle-down intellectualism of Marcuse and Horkheimer might have worked on a college level, where students substituted professors for parents as authority figures and felt liberated by their new, less stodgy, "be yourself" quasi-parents, but it took the brilliance of an Alinsky to bring the Marcuse Marxist creed to the common man by fooling him into thinking it was purely American. It took Alinsky's thug tactics to enervate the happy, healthy American middle class and get them to accept major changes to the status quo, and to mobilize the racial and sexual identity groups that Marcuse needed to substitute for the generally complacent middle class. It took Alinsky to shut up the opposition using the methodologies of political correctness, to frighten people into submission and create an informal anti–First Amendment regime where if you speak out, you become a personal target. It took Alinsky to put the Complex totally into effect. Every successful interest group and social movement in the United States since the 1960s has used Frankfurt School ideology and Alinsky rules.

It's tragic it has taken conservatives so long to realize it.

CHAPTER 7

Pragmatic Primer for Realistic Revolutionaries

After I wrote *Hollywood, Interrupted*, and as I was helping create a conservative Hollywood network and creating the barrel full of liberal eggs that is the Huffington Post, I felt good. My journey into the culture wars had begun auspiciously. We were making strides by using the left against itself at the Huffington Post and by creating a conservative underground in Hollywood.

But I hadn't been tested by fire. I hadn't felt the pressure cooker. I hadn't put myself out in the open.

What would happen once I forayed into the bright sunlight of public scrutiny and faced the music?

I was about to find out.

In March 2005, I got invited to appear on the HBO program *Real Time with Bill Maher*.

At the time, the left was starting to get its sea legs in terms of framing the Iraq War as illegitimate and President Bush as a heinous commander in chief. I knew the audience would be composed of Maher's loyalists, the MoveOn.org plants. It wasn't my first time before a studio audience—I'd done the *Dennis Miller Show* many times—but this was my first time before a hostile studio audience.

It went relatively well. I defended Bush on the war, which made me performer non grata, but I also got off a couple of one-liners, especially one mitigating the concern that people were having about teenage boys having sex with attractive twentysomething teachers. At the time, there was a spate of those things happening, and I said something predictable that your average red-blooded male would say, explaining that there's a double standard and a fundamental difference between a teenage girl having sex with her older male teacher, and a teenage boy having sex with his hot female teacher. It was a throwaway line that in my mind ameliorated my presence on the panel, a line that conveyed that I wasn't one of those stodgy conservatives.

I got off the show after having been fearful of the audience and Maher pummeling me, and I had survived, without a problem. *Maybe I'll get invited back again*, I thought to myself. At the postparty,

I received universal plaudits from the crew, and I was treated like a regular citizen by Bill Maher and by an actor from *The West Wing*. It felt good to be patted on the back instead of being treated like a pariah. I was riding high.

The following Monday, I got a call from a friend of mine, a closeted conservative Hollywood filmmaker.

"I saw your appearance," he told me. "Why didn't you stand up for what you believed in?"

It was the deepest cut, because in the recesses of my mind I was fully aware that I had gone on Maher's show wanting desperately to be liked instead of trying to make my best case. I realized that I talked a mean game, and I thought a mean game, and I gave a lot of people great talking points and great ideas, but I'd spent too much time thinking about the persona I could craft for myself that I and my family could bear while living in the middle of West Los Angeles, the heart of the beast.

For the next four years, that Maher appearance gnawed at me. I had been flirting with acting like myself in public, but I was still afraid. Sometimes in the midst of my sleep pattern I would wake up from nightmares in a cold sweat, one thought running through my mind: what if I went in front of the public and got booed? What if they rejected me? It became a constant, growing fear in my life.

Am I going to be who I am, I asked myself, *or am I going to craft a more sophisticated yet untruthful public persona where I pull my punches?*

Then, in March 2009, I was asked to be on Maher's show again. It was at the beginning of the Obama administration, the height of the Hope Brigade and the Change Parade, and there was every opportunity to be an accommodationist. Even moderate conservatives were still telling their followers to give Obama a chance.

I knew Obama, and I knew he didn't deserve a chance to turn America into a Frankfurt School dystopia. He was a Frankfurt School scholar, a Marxist gradualist in moderate's clothing, a community organizer in the Alinsky mold. But I wasn't sure that I wanted to stake out that position with Bill Maher. Perhaps they even invited me on because I had complied with the rules of the game back in 2005.

When I arrived at the studio, my adrenaline started flowing. I had forgotten how much trepidation comes up by doing a show like *Real Time*, where you go to a CBS soundstage and they bring you to your dressing room, where they give you a jacket of the show and a fruit basket, where they delicately dress you up with makeup and make you feel like an actual member of the glitterati. It's an intoxicating sensation. It's validating. But don't be deceived.

Being invited on *Real Time with Bill Maher* is the quickest way to kick in the groin any past perception of inferiority. You know you're going to sneak up onto HBO and an ex-girlfriend or a high-school bully or a teacher who gave you a D is going to be there, and sitting on that stage is a giant "Screw you" to all of them. The narcissism is appealing—but the problem is that you're only affirmed in your narcissism if you buy into the system, if you get the cheap laughs and convince the audience to love you.

Again, I was faced with a choice. I could appeal to the composite audience, which was a conglomeration of all the insecurities of my childhood and young adulthood, saying, *Hey, look, I've arrived, I'm on television—and what's more, I got the host to laugh!* Or I could appeal to my true conscience.

In the green room, I greeted the staffers I remembered from the last time and spent time preparing with Maher's longtime executive producer, Scott Carter, an old-school liberal with an immense respect for difference of opinion. I met Professor Michael Eric Dyson, and I started to piece together what the show was going to be like. I knew who he was—*Hey, that's Cornel West Jr.! You're the guy who speaks in iambic pentameter def poetry slam clichés. Prepackaged speechifications that nobody understands. Oh, brother!*—and I realized that they weren't even having a third panelist who could alleviate the tension with a joke. I recognized that Maher, with political correctness on his side and as his chief weapon, was going to use Michael Eric Dyson to frame me as the racial Other, as the oppressor himself or, at the very least, as the unwitting aider and abettor of the oppressor.

We walked out onto the stage, or rather, onto the stage behind the stage, as Bill was beginning the show. I stood on the secondary set waiting for the discussion to begin, in the dark, next to Michael Eric Dyson. I was thinking only one thing: *Stand up for what you believe in this time. Stand up for what you believe in this time. Stand up for what you believe in this time. Don't divert into comedy mode. Don't take the easiest pathway out of this experience. Stand up for what you believe in.*

It was an incredibly committed moment in my life. I knew I was going to go out there and face down an audience predetermined to hate my guts, Bill Maher predetermined to make mincemeat out of me using his winks, looks, nods, dismissive gestures, and comedy to make me the outsider. And I knew I wasn't going to run away this time behind my shield of jocularity and submission.

The bell rang, and it became obvious very quickly that this wasn't going to be the kind of fight where the two boxers tiptoed around the canvas looking for openings, testing the opponent's commitment to the match. The rumble began immediately. And I was right—the audience was predisposed toward hating me. And Bill's eyes, from the very outset, asked me, *Why are you even here?* despite the fact that he had invited me.

I made an opening joke, which the audience dismissed without laughter. Then Maher introduced Dyson—big applause. He introduced me—tepid applause. And I thought to myself: *Screw it. Go for it.*

Maher opened by asking me whether Republicans were just being obstructionist. I answered that the party was in disarray, and Obama was providing a great opportunity for Republicans to decide what they stand for. I said that we couldn't look at Bush as an example of how America should be headed—he had been a big-government advocate, too. I pointed out that Americans ought to look to the libertarian movement in terms of a small-government program, and I cited the fact that Ayn Rand's books were flying off of the bookshelves.

That's when it got nasty. Maher immediately claimed that ammo was flying off the shelves, too, because Americans were afraid of Obama and his "Negro army," implying that red states full of rednecks were all angry racists. I didn't let him get away with it. I knew that he had gone there because he was lazy, because the reactionary racial politics of the left dictates that when they have no evidence, they throw out the racism charge.

"Where's this racism coming from? I haven't seen it online," I asked Maher.

"Well, the racism is coming from Rush Limbaugh," Maher answered. His audience of MoveOn.org-trained seals applauded him. It was another lazy move on his part.

I knew that he had gone there because he'd likely never listened to Rush Limbaugh, because I *used to be part of that crowd.* And Maher knew that across the table from him he had Michael Eric Dyson, who was going to reaffirm his points.

"Whoa, whoa, whoa," I interrupted. "I find that offensive. There's nothing in this country that is a worse accusation. It's where in America, if you accuse somebody of racism, that person has to disprove that. It is completely un-American to call him racist—you tell me what he [Limbaugh] has said that is racist. The man has been on the air for twenty-one years, fifteen hours a week...."

Bill pointed to Michael Eric Dyson, his tag-team partner in this matter. And on cue, Dyson answered: "I'll just tell you, first of all, Rush Limbaugh seems to have a problem with black guys who run things. Think about it. So he was jumping on Donovan McNabb for being a black quarterback.... He got pushed off the air.... Now he's jumping on Obama."

At which point Bill jumped in: "He's said a lot of racist things."

"No, he hasn't," I said.

Then Dyson jumped in again. "He's not saying that 'I hate Negroes' specifically; what he's doing is creating an atmosphere of such profound vitriol and hatred and, I think, denunciation of black people and of the ideas associated with those people who are vulnerable, that yeah, there is a strong implication about black people going on there. And if you put Rush Limbaugh in the context of the monkey appearing in the cartoon in the *New York Post*..."

I sat back in my chair. "For crying out loud," I muttered.

"It's code language!" Dyson insisted.

"No, it isn't code language," I said. "There's no greater defender of Clarence Thomas than Rush Limbaugh." The MoveOn.org crowd laughed on cue, and I thanked them as such.

Bill stepped in again. "Clarence Thomas, a black man who does not represent ninety-five percent of black people." The crowd cheered.

"That's bullshit," I insisted. "You're allowed to have independent thought in this country, and this type of intimidation by the Black Studies intelligentsia crowd that intimidates black people who are conservative...That's why I became conservative."

Dyson went on another iambic pentameter def poetry slam filibuster for the next three minutes. There was simply no way to stop him. Critical-theory phrases flowed from his mouth like water from a fountain. He babbled about institutional injustice. He called Clarence Thomas a ventriloquist dummy for white supremacy. He called Obama a black man in public housing. I started to answer. And Maher cut me off: "I will let you answer, but I just want to say, that is some motherfucking articulateness!" And the audience, of course, clapped wildly.

Then I brought out my best skill: researching. I had done my Lexis-Nexis searching before the program—I knew that somebody was likely to attack Rush that week, since the Obama Complex had put Rush in its Alinsky crosshairs that week. I also knew that back around 9/11, Maher had made some controversial comments that got him boycotted in several markets, and that Rush had defended him. So before the show, I e-mailed Rush and asked him about it. "Yes," Rush told me, "I even received a handwritten thank-you note from Bill Maher."

"Let me end on this note," I said. "Back in 2001,

when you were attacked by two yahoos down in Houston when you said what you said on *Politically Incorrect*, it was a Republican establishment, it was Rush Limbaugh, Sean Hannity, Michael Medved, [and] Dennis Prager who came to your defense, and you sent Rush Limbaugh a letter, a note thanking him for this." You could actually sense the air go out of the room as the audience stared at Maher, *Holy shit!* written over each and every face. "You're part of the bullying tactic," I continued. "Calling a person a racist is the worst thing you can call somebody in this country."

Maher was silent. I could see he wanted to reach across the table and strangle me. Finally he answered, weakly, "You're saying that if I actually think he has racist tendencies, that's off-limits—"

Now I cut him off. "What racist tendencies?"

And Maher answered: "He sang 'Barack the Magic Negro.'"

My heart leaped with joy. I had suspected that Maher would bring up "Barack the Magic Negro," and once again, I had done my research—thank God Arianna had hired me under those false pretenses. "Barack the Magic Negro" was a parody song Rush had based on a column of the same title by leftist *Los Angeles Times* columnist David Ehrenstein, an absurdist essay in which he sarcastically praised Obama as an ethereal, magical black man who could perform political wizardry because of his intellect and mixed racial heritage. Maher clearly didn't know what he was talking about.

It devolved from there. Maher asked a question about stem cells and Dyson delivered stem-cell iambic pentameter def poetry slam filibuster remix. I cut through the crap with prepackaged talking points I had cribbed from the estimable Charles Krauthammer, whose work on the subject seemed eminently plagiarizable. It stopped them in their tracks. If they had asked one follow-up question, of course, I would have fallen to the ground in a puddle of water and curled up in a fetal position and admitted I didn't know what the hell I was talking about. But they didn't. I even challenged his audience at one point when they booed me before I was able to finish my sentence. Even Maher reacted; his Achilles' heel is that even though he's a leftie, he exhibits clear contempt for the astroturfed audience he relies upon for his laughs.

The awkwardness continued for a full, commercial-free half hour, defusing the show's usual comedic touch.[1] As I walked offstage, comedian Sarah Silverman passed by me on her way onstage without making eye contact, but she did touch Professor Dyson on the arm and tell him he was amazing. She then sat down in the chair I

had been sitting in, looked down, swiped the tab-
letop, and for comedic effect said to Maher and his
MoveOn audience, "It's icky here."

I walked back to my dressing room, passing the
same staffers who had greeted me amicably before
the show but who were now looking at me like I
had just passed gas at their dinner table. Back in
my dressing room, I was received by horror-stricken
family and friends. Their collective look was one of
being at a loss for words to console me. To them, it
was clear that I had been set up.

My BlackBerry started to overflow with texts and
e-mails. Dwight Schultz, who played "Howling
Mad" Murdock on the hit '80s show *The A-Team*,
was the only one who immediately saw things the
way I did. The verdict was otherwise unanimous,
and everybody was trying to put the best spin on
what appeared to be a horrific car crash of a show.
A veteran comedy writer friend of mine who is a
longtime Maher aficionado reminds me to this day
that it was by far the strangest episode of the show
he ever watched. Even Maher had clearly been
thrown off his game.

I felt something different: an almost druglike
and ethereal and divine exultation. Recognition
that I had been born, publicly and politically, for
the first time. It was like looking into a mirror and
recognizing, *This is who I am. I'm not going to*

tap-dance around what I believe in anymore. Even though I had secretly believed in conservative ideas, and even though I had used different tactics to push them, and even though I had insinuated my ideas into the marketplace and effectively circumvented the Complex by contributing to the New Media, I had never been willing to stick my neck out like Rush Limbaugh or Ann Coulter or Sean Hannity. I had never been willing to stand out there and be the object of public ridicule. I had feared what it would be like, feared what retribution would come, feared what the social consternation would be, feared what the swords and the slings and the arrows and the rocks upon my body would feel like, feared a comedienne whose work I enjoyed mocking me in her presence. I had feared in both my waking and sleeping hours what it would be like.

And now, walking out of the Maher show, I realized that what I had feared most—expulsion and derision—didn't really even hurt, not when you are standing up for what you believe. I raised my Cactus Cooler in honor of the individual who came up with the aphorism "That which doesn't kill you makes you stronger." Nietzsche, by the way. I realized that while adulation has its moments and can be like a bath in warm water after coming in from a snowstorm, the psychic high from standing up for

what you believe in and being attacked for it far sur-
passed the comfort to be derived from that bath of
praise.

I had passed what I call the Coulter Threshold:
the point where you understand that Ann Coulter
and those like her are standing up for what they believe in, feeling the righteousness of living without
fear of missing a dinner invite from Tina Brown or
fund-raisers with Steve Capus or Ben Sherwood or
Steven Spielberg or Jeffrey Katzenberg—or worse,
the agony of being excoriated by those conservatives who fret that their liberal overlords will start
admonishing them for keeping company with you.
Feeling the thrill of sending a message to these
people that we reject their worldview the way they
reject ours.

I want to bottle that and get it out to every American. I want to teach everyone I know that there's
nothing to fear but fear itself, and that there's strength
in numbers. I've been looking directly forward instead of into the rearview mirror, not worrying about
what people think about me, and it has empowered
me. And it can empower you. Not only can you take
assaults, you can weather them and be strengthened
by them—and gain the power to punch back, to go
on the offensive. Our opponents have spent so many
years on the offensive with people lying prone at their
feet that they've forgotten what it's like to be on the

defensive. If we come after them, they won't know how to respond.

My transformation from empty-headed, pop-culture-infused, talking-points-parroting liberal to New Media warrior took me four decades. But those years in the wilderness taught me some basic rules that I have applied steadily and steadfastly, and that are bearing tremendous results. Before we get to the application of the tactics, and before I lay out my game plan for the next few years, let's summarize the rules every conservative activist needs to use when fighting the left:

1. **Don't be afraid to go into enemy territory.** This is perhaps the most important rule you'll read in this book, and the one most likely to be ignored by the Republican Party and the Old Guard in the conservative movement. They would say I shouldn't have appeared on Maher, because it was an audience stacked against me. But that's the same mentality that led the right to abandon Hollywood, academia, and the media—and the effects have been disastrous. The right figures that talk radio, Fox News, and some independent Internet sites will allow us to distribute our ideas to the masses. There's one problem: *those outlets are exponentially outnumbered and out-*

gunned by the Complex. They're Alinsky-ed by
the activist left, which insists Fox News is Faux
News and talk radio is hate radio. Obama is
leading the charge, targeting specific hosts and
specific outlets. Remember Rush Limbaugh? Or
their insistence that Fox News isn't a real news
outlet like CNN or MSNBC?

The problem is that it works with the vast
majority of apolitical voters in America. In my
neighborhood, our strategy of disengagement
isn't working too well. People who don't watch
Fox News or listen to Rush have strong, defiant,
negative opinions about those outlets, just like
I did when I was a liberal. I'd never listened
to Rush in my life, but I knew—I knew!—that
Rush was the epitome of evil. I knew, just as
the Complex wanted me to know, that Rush
was a racist, sexist, homophobic bigot that only
KKKers listened to while driving their broken-
down pickups and drinking moonshine.

The army of the emboldened and gleefully ill-
informed is growing. Groupthink happens, and
we have to take it head-on. We can't win the
political war until we win the cultural war. The
Frankfurt School knew that—that's why they
won the cultural war and then, on its back, the
political war. We can do the same, but we have
to be willing to enter the arena. By neglecting

The View or, worse, by ignoring Jon Stewart, Stephen Colbert, Maher, and David Letterman—we allow them to distort and demean us as they romanticize and elevate themselves. It's harder to attack people to their faces than behind their backs, and we have to confront them face-to-face. Young people suckle at the teat of pop culture—but by refusing to fight for their attention, we lose by default.

Our most articulate voices, likable faces, and best idea-makers need to go into hostile territory and plant the seeds of doubt in our ideological enemy and the apolitical masses who simply go with the media flow. Our babysitter has an Obama bumper sticker on her car, but admits she knows nothing about politics. How did that happen? It's what the Complex tells her to do to be cool. We have to use their media control against them by walking into the lion's den, heads held high, proud of who we are and what we stand for.

There's no time to continue backing away. If we're standing still, we're moving backward. Get in the game. Get in the fight.

2. **Expose the left for who they are—in their own words.** It's easy to label the left, to analyze them, to take them apart using your rationality—their program fails every time it's tried, and their lex-

icon, once you know it, is as predictable as the sun rising in the east. What's much harder than understanding the left is exposing it.

That's where citizen journalists come in. Drudge was a citizen journalist, and he took on a president. Today, we all have the power to be citizen journalists via the Internet—there's no Complex gatekeeper to stop us from posting the truth about enemies of freedom and liberty in this country. In the past few years alone, citizen journalists have deposed Dan Rather for his scurrilous and baseless attacks on George W. Bush; exposed John Kerry's true war record during the 2004 election cycle; debunked Reuters's photography fraud in the Middle East; raised the question whether Barack Obama's autobiography, *Dreams from My Father*, was ghostwritten by domestic terrorist Bill Ayers; gotten rid of communist Van Jones; and the list goes on. The Internet has become the shining beacon of journalistic freedom, tearing apart congressional bills piece by piece for the benefit of the public, even when our own legislators won't read them.

The key to the success of the New Media, though, is making news by breaking news. And that means that conservatives need to use their new best technological friends: the MP3 recorder, the phone camera, and the blogosphere.

It's one thing to say that the left likes socialism, but it's a real story to get Barack Obama to admit it on camera, as he did to Joe the Plumber during the 2008 election cycle. Video journalism is the most potent kind of journalism. We live in an age of sound and sight, not text, and we have to adapt to that age.

You are the soldiers in this war against the Institutional Left. You have been issued your weapons. Go out and use them. Make it impossible for the Complex to ignore you.

3. **Be open about your secrets.** If you're going to go out in public, be absolutely open about what you've done in the past. Take a page from Barack Obama, who revealed in his probably Ayers-ghostwritten autobiography[2] that he had done a bit of blow, and hung out with commies and assorted lowlifes. Once it was out there, there wasn't much that the right could do with it—he'd already admitted it.

By way of contrast, take a look at Mark Foley. If he'd admitted he was gay right off the bat, the left wouldn't have had much to pillory him with. The left never gets cited for hypocrisy (see Clinton, Bill), but the right is cited with it all the time because we actually have standards. That means we have to out ourselves before the

left does it for us. In this book, I've already admitted to libertine sensibilities that were taken
to absurd heights during my collegiate stint in
New Orleans. I am not a Puritan. Frankly, John
Waters's movies and Johnny Knoxville's *Jackass*
series are more up my alley than Mel Gibson's
The Passion of the Christ. The days of the left
forcing us into a small, monolithic, and mono-
chromatic box are over, and we have to fight
their caricature of us.

Actually, George W. Bush did the same thing
during the 2000 election. "When I was young
and stupid, I was young and stupid," he said.
Once he had come clean, the left was stuck—
they couldn't do anything.

Hypocrisy is such a powerful argument for the
left because it appeals directly to the emotional
heart of politics: one standard for you, another
for me. It's no wonder Alinsky relied heavily on
his rule 4: Make the enemy live up to their own
book of rules. We have more rules than they do
with regard to morality, which means we have to
live up to them more often. But mistakes in the
past don't need to be skeletons waiting to come
out of the closet. If you've made mistakes, reveal
them at the first available opportunity. Embrace
those mistakes. Don't talk about how you regret
them—talk about how you lived through them

and how they made you who you are today. Embracing your mistakes makes you invulnerable to their slings.

Just don't screw up badly *now*.

4. **Don't let the Complex use its PC lexicon to characterize you and shape the narrative.** If you've got a big story, the Complex will do what it always does: attack you personally using the PC lexicon. You immediately become a racist, sexist, homophobic, jingoistic nativist. Don't let them do it. The fact is this: if you refuse to buy into their lexicon, if you refuse to back down in the face of those intimidation tactics, they can't harm you. You're Neo in the hallway with Agent Smith after he figures out that the Complex is a sham—the spoon isn't bending, he's bending. Once it hits him that he's not bound by the rules of the game, he can literally stop bullets. You can stop their bullets because their bullets *aren't real*.

Leftist assassins like Max Blumenthal, a one-trick hit man, have tried to label me and many of my allies as racists. I don't let them get away with it. I don't just call them out, I make sure that my righteous indignation registers on the Richter scale. I don't pull out my record on civil rights or my black friends. I simply point out that what they're doing is pure Alinsky and that it has no basis in fact or reality, and that they're showing themselves to be racists in their own right by citing race every time they meet someone with whom they disagree.

While I was at the 2010 CPAC, I was confronted by Daryle Jenkins of the One People's Project based on my defense of James O'Keefe—he had been slandered online as a racist by Blumenthal because he had attended a conference at the Georgetown Law Center that included racist Jared Taylor, John Derbyshire of *National Review* (who ripped into Taylor for his racism during the forum), and African-American conservative Kevin Martin. At the event, O'Keefe sided with Derbyshire and Martin against Taylor.

Anyway, here's how the incident went down:

Breitbart: Max Blumenthal is a political hit man. What he does is he rapes the reputation of people mercilessly. He makes scurrilous, unsupportable accusations against people and he smears them using the political correctness he learned so well in the post-modern academy and the politics of personal destruction he learned firsthand from his father, Sid "Vicious" Blumenthal. He destroys people. He isol-

eck Out Receipt

land Park Public Library Branch
8-428-5100
.orlandparklibrary.org

urday, November 17, 2018 12:33:43 PM

m: 31315004024183
le: Righteous indignation : excuse me w
e I save the world!
1 no.: LT 302.23093 BRE
erial: Book
: 12/08/2018

al items: 1

just saved $30.00 by using your librar
oday. You have saved $320.00 this year
$340.00 since you began using the Pola
Library system!

Orland Park Public Library named one o
llinois 200 Great Places.

DUE ON
26 Dec

ates threats to the reign of the far left and the reign of his father's cabal of Clinton/ Podesta and the organized left. He's a vicious guy. He falsely slandered James O'Keefe as a racist, we disproved it—

Jenkins: How did you disprove it, sir?

Breitbart: I'm being interviewed right here.

Jenkins: I'm the one who put that story out first.

Breitbart: Well, then, you suck.

Jenkins: You're lying. You're lying.... He was at that white supremacist forum.

Breitbart: It wasn't a white supremacist forum.

Jenkins: Yes it was!

Breitbart: Then why was Kevin Martin there?

At this point, Jenkins started pointing his finger inches from my face and moving his face close to mine. It then devolved into a series of accusations by Jenkins regarding details of the event. Finally, Jenkins got to his point:

Breitbart: Are you accusing me of being a white supremacist?

Jenkins: I'm accusing you of being a racist, yes I am.

Breitbart: Okay, have a nice day, buddy.
Will somebody please take this guy out of
here? You punk.

That was it. Jenkins walked away.

The key to the conversation was that I didn't start defending myself against his baseless charge of racism. I dismissed it out of hand as ridiculous because it *was* ridiculous. He *was* a punk for leveling that kind of charge without any basis whatsoever. I don't let my enemies characterize me without any evidence, and you shouldn't let them characterize you. Name-calling is their best strategy, and if you don't lend it credence, and instead force them to back up their charges with specifics, you win. *Revel* in the name-calling—it means you've got them reduced to their lowest, basest tactic, and the one that carries the least weight if you refuse to abide by their definition of you.

5. **Control your own story—don't let the Complex do it.** A one-and-done story isn't worth anything. One fact can be posted on the Internet and flushed down the memory hole faster than anyone can imagine. How many incredible pieces of journalistic revelation have been lost because they weren't properly presented to the public?

Serialization is good. Van Jones was taken down by Glenn Beck because Beck had the goods—and because he revealed them piece by piece. He got Jones and his defenders to come out of the closet and attack him. Then he calmly laid his cards on the table, one by one.

It's the same strategy I saw Arianna pursue during the Larry Lawrence scandal. People came out of the woodwork to attack her as a scurrilous human being slandering a dead war hero. And she smiled and let them come at her. Then she put her evidence into the public eye, bit by bit, keeping the story alive. Feeding the media is like training a dog—you can't throw an entire steak at a dog to train it to sit. You have to give it little bits of steak over and over and over again until it learns its lesson. That's what Arianna did.

It's the exact same thing Drudge did with Lewinsky. He broke the story in pieces rather than in a long essay laying out all the facts, and he didn't let the media's cries for him to reveal all his information control his decision-making process. Instead, he controlled the media.

The important thing to remember here is that the media are like a leech hanging on the back of the news makers, and the news makers have every right and ability to feed that leech little by little instead of letting it suck them dry all at once. Keep your story alive by planning its release down to the minutest detail.

6. **Ubiquity is key.** As a capitalist and as a web publisher, pageviews are certainly a desired commodity. But when playing for political or cultural keeps, impact matters most. And, when ABCNBCCBSCNNMSNBC and the dailies are working against you and ignoring you, ubiquity is a key weapon. That means developing relationships with like-minded allies or even enemies and news junkies and allowing them to share in the good fortune of a good scoop.

While the crux of a story can be weaponized and launched on one of my websites, there are often peripheral angles that can be developed elsewhere with a separate but related media life of their own. For instance, the ACORN story was unbelievably complex. A key component of exposing the scandal was a detailed analysis of ACORN's structure and its past scandals. I knew legal minds were needed to weigh in on these aspects. Patrick Frey, who runs the indispensable Patterico website, created a parallel line of attack, not just against ACORN, but against its myriad defenders, who lied and misdirected to try to kill the story. The ACORN story couldn't have been the success it was without others—

talk radio and alternative news outlets that were invested in the story and could deliver scoops of their own. So, I planted scoops with what business school types would call my "competitors," and I watched the story explode, my pageviews go through the roof, and my brand flourish. Sometimes the best ideas are counterintuitive.

I love living in Los Angeles and not DC, because in DC there are too many fighting over too little ground for their own fifteen minutes. The scarcity mentality is strangling the growth of the conservative movement. From outside DC, I can see that ubiquity is about growing the pie for everyone, spreading the stories, the channels of distribution, the resources around so that the entire movement can benefit, because our chunk of the public square gets bigger and bigger each time we break something huge.

7. **Engage in the social arena.** My first instinct about Facebook was my first instinct about Twitter was my first instinct about MySpace. I was right about MySpace—it sucks. I was definitely wrong about Facebook and Twitter.

Using my "ubiquity" rule, the citizen journalist isn't always reporting in the ledes, headlines, and paragraphs form. Sometimes a tweet or a retweet can grant an idea more legs. Sometimes a status update can lead to the mother lode. Yes, there are slick advisers falsely promising a social networking Gold Rush, but a well-socially-networked person can soon carry more weight than a household-name columnist at your local news daily.

Building a movement used to take time, but now it can be done in a few hours with the right connections and the right posts on the right websites. Take, for one example, flash mobs. These are gatherings spawned over the Internet on hours' notice, and they gather thousands of people, whether it's for snowball fights or for rioting in the streets of Philadelphia.

The Tea Parties have used the power of social media to get their message out there in a new and incredible way. There are no leaders to the Tea Party, which is a great thing, and there's no formal program to the Tea Party—it's truly a party of the people, and originally, it was based on conservative people partying. If any liberal attended a Tea Party event, they'd be shocked to see that it isn't a KKK rally; it's a social gathering of thousands of like-minded people of all races and ages, people looking for others who believe in the same values.

It's also particularly true in Hollywood, where socializing is the basis of business. That's why

I've tried to put people in Hollywood together, and it's already spawning actual creative projects. Seek out other people and build an army.

8. **Don't pretend to know more than you do.** This one trips up conservatives all the time. We want to argue policy because when we know policy, there's no way they can beat us, because all they have is their lexicon of name-calling and societal expulsion. We have reason on our side.

But just because we have reason on our side doesn't mean that everyone is equipped to be Charles Krauthammer or Michael Barone, policy wonks who can pull facts from the Office of Management and Budget out of every orifice. Most of us aren't experts on the latest budget package or stem-cell line regulation, but that doesn't mean we're powerless—it means we get to play Socrates, asking pointed questions rather than citing facts we may not be sure of.

One of the low points of my media life was getting a call after the nomination of John Roberts for the United States Supreme Court. A producer from CNN's now-cancelled Aaron Brown show asked me to go on TV and discuss the wisdom of President Bush's choice. I remember taking a Civil Liberties course at Tulane in summer school. As I recall there was a case called *Mapp v. Ohio.* That was the extent of my then-qualification to pontificate on such legal matters. I am not sure what demoralized me more: that I was asked to do so by a leading cable news network, or that I readily accepted. Had Wikipedia not been invented, I would have had nothing to say. But I did, and I survived. My takeaway from the revealing moment about the low standards for TV punditry was that if I valued my career, I would only accept media invites where I could dictate the terms of engagement (i.e., bring my own stories, my own perspectives, etc.) or where I could change the subject to war footing.

By avoiding talking about that which I do not know, perhaps I limit my ability to appear on more shows. But I definitely limit my ability to screw up.

Put another way: don't be the guy with a knife at the gunfight. It rarely ends well.

9. **Don't let them pretend to know more than they do.** This is really the converse of the last rule. Your opponents will pretend to be experts if you don't, but that's okay, because you can always puncture their balloon with one word: *why.* Asking them to provide evidence for their assertions is always fun, and it's even more fun asking them to provide the sources for that evidence.

Attacking the fundamental basis of their arguments is fun, too—if they tell you health care is a right, for example, ask why. Liberals don't have a why, other than their own utopianism and their dyspeptic view of the status quo and America. Reason is not their strong suit—emotion is. Force them to play on the football field of reason.

10. **Ridicule is man's most potent weapon.** Here, Alinsky and I agree. It's the truest of Alinsky's statements, and it's the most effective. Tina Fey, not the MSM, sullied Sarah Palin's image. Chevy Chase brought down Gerald Ford. Jon Stewart brought down Bush.

    And we'll bring down Obama, but not unless we're willing to get unserious. Stuffy old white guys wearing bow ties and talking about the danger of national deficits don't get much done—talented people who can translate political chaos into merry pranksterism do.

11. **Don't let them get away with ignoring their own rules.** Alinsky is right again. They set up this PC Complex, and they have to be held accountable to it, if only for honesty's sake, and we're the only ones who will do it. Joe Biden is still vice president of the United States even

though he called the first black president "clean" and "articulate." Harry Reid is still Senate majority leader even though he said Obama was "light-skinned" and could drop his "Negro dialect" on cue. Until his death in 2010, Senator Robert Byrd was "a lion of the Senate" even though he was a former Kleagle in the KKK. If these had been Republicans, they would have been hounded from office. They're Democrats, so they're not.

But that doesn't mean we can't hold them responsible for breaching their own standards. Every time they say things like this, we need to force them to back down and apologize, and we can't allow their allies to let them off the hook with excuses about how they stand for the right policies. Frankfurt School tactics can't work here—standing for liberalism doesn't mean you're allowed to violate the conventions of PC. At the very least, we need to force these hypocrites to stand up against their own PC regime in order to defend themselves.

12. **Truth isn't mean. It's truth.** I know that some of you are feeling rotten about using some of these tactics. We can ignore the tactics, but the left will continue to use them to their benefit; just as the Frankfurt School relied on the good nature

and honesty of Americans who wouldn't engage in un-Christian tactics in order to achieve their massive victory, the left continues to rely on our honesty and aboveboard good nature in order to achieve theirs.

We can't let them.

We start by uncovering the truth and telling everyone about it. I'm not religious, and I'm certainly no theologian, but if there is one thing in religion that speaks to me, it is the idea of absolute truth. In fact, the word *truth* has meaning only if it is absolute. And absolute truth will set us all free from the grip of the Complex, because the Complex lives in the clouds, in the theoretical heavens—the Frankfurt School was successful only because they were able to shift Marxism's basis from real-world predictions to descriptions of supposed historical processes, making Marxism unfalsifiable. We have to falsify their theory by presenting unvarnished truth after unvarnished truth until the light dawns on everyone just how right we are.

13. **Believe in the audacity of hope.** It's too bad President Obama is such a joyless, politically correct automaton, because he's terrifically agile with his prepared words. To paraphrase his victory speech after the 2008 election, the rise of

the New Media alone is not the change we seek—it is only the chance for us to make that change. And that cannot happen if we go back to the way things were. It cannot happen without you.

It can't happen without hope for America and faith in its people—two things Obama and his leftist ilk don't have, which is why they try to shut it down in others. We have the power to unravel the Complex and destroy the Institutional Left. It won't be easy. It will take time and effort, and there will be false starts and roadblocks, but we'll do it, because we have to do it. Apathy in the face of determined Frankfurt School/Alinsky/critical-theory-trained activists is national suicide.

These are some of my basic rules. Now you'll see how a small group of people put these rules into action and took down one of the biggest and most powerful political organizations in the United States using a short skirt, a hidden camera, and the power of the Internet.

CHAPTER 8

The Abu Ghraib of the Great Society

I met James O'Keefe in June 2009. James came to me at the behest of Maura Flynn, a friend and libertarian documentary producer in Virginia. I had met Maura back in 2004 when she was the associate producer of *Michael Moore Hates America*, a film to which I contributed analysis (and which allowed me to heap scorn on this engorged cicada who appears every three years or so to suck the life force from his countrymen). Maura and I are about the same age, and we are both driven by an appreciation for the sheer power of America's pop culture. We both also obsess that conservatives are stuck in a nineteenth-century media strategy that will lose elections in perpetuity if they don't wake up to the fact that those geeky graduate students generating the latest apps and networks won't "rule the world someday"—they already *do*.

So when Maura called to tell me about a new find of hers, I knew I'd better take it seriously. Maura was always bringing me up-and-coming conservatives (people like the ballsy Evan Coyne Maloney, director of the documentary *Indoctrinate U*), and her excitement over the phone got my attention.

Well, sort of. As is often the case, I was focused on three other things simultaneously, eyeing the television while handling the remote and my Black-Berry. Luckily, Maura plays my ADHD to perfection, and she cut in: "Andrew, I'm serious! This guy's stuff is unbelievable! He goes into ACORN as a pimp, with a girl as a prostitute, and they *help him*."

That woke me up. "Really?"

"Really. And it's *on film*."

"Is it good?"

"It's *very* good. He's coming out to California. You've gotta meet him."

A couple of weeks later, on Friday, August 7, 2009, James showed up at my house. When he walked through the door, the first thing I thought was *This is Matthew Modine from* Vision Quest, *after he sweated himself into the lower weight division for high-school wrestling*. He was tall and thin, and the resemblance was uncanny. My next thought was: *This guy decided to take on ACORN?*

I took him down to the basement, and we talked for a while, getting to know each other. I then called in my business partner, Larry Solov. Larry is your typically skeptical lawyer, who was there to protect me from committing myself to questionable projects. Hunter S. Thompson had Oscar; I've got Larry. I knew that if I was going to invest time and effort in something, I needed Larry to see it, too—I needed Larry to let me know whether I could trust my eyes.

James showed me the video from the Baltimore office of ACORN.

My jaw dropped.

The video showed James repeatedly proclaiming that he was running a prostitution ring, that he and his "partner" were going to be "turning tricks" in the house for which he wanted ACORN's tax advice, and that he was going to be importing underage prostitutes from El Salvador. The videos left no doubt in any rational viewer's mind whether the ACORN employees misunderstood the proposition. It was like watching Western civilization fall off a cliff. Even Larry, whose heart beats about six times a minute, was stunned.

I knew it was the goods—but I also knew something else. So when the video ended, I took James outside the basement into my backyard, which overlooks the Los Angeles National Ce-

metery. We looked over the rows and rows of grave-
stones. It was a peaceful, serene setting, and we
contemplated each other for a moment before I
asked him: Just what the hell are you up to here?

James, it turns out, was a Rutgers University
graduate, a former philosophy student driven by
a singular mission: to create a whole new school
of challenging, provocative filmmaking. What's so
unique about that, you ask? Unlike every other
"media provocateur" you've ever heard lionized in
the *New Yorker*, James's target was the Institutional
Left. Charming, confident, a born prankster with
mischief in his eye, this reedy Irishman had been
punking the entrenched orthodoxies since his Rutgers days.[*] All he cared about—what he was con-
sumed with—was finding a way to keep doing it.
"Would you be willing to buy this?" he asked me
about the ACORN tapes.

It was now that I had to tell him the "something

---

[*]You might recall one of James's college stunts. To
highlight the Kafkaesque extremes of political correctness Rutgers had descended into, James, of Irish
descent, decided to complain to the college administration about the serving of Lucky Charms cereal in
the school cafeteria. The school agreed, pulling the
"offensive" cereal with that "degrading" leprechaun
on the box from its shelves.

else" I knew. I was only glad James would hear it from me. "James, the footage is awesome, and what's more, important," I told him—his eyes lit up—"unfortunately, I don't think it is worth a red cent." I explained to him that there just wasn't a market (yet!) for conservative product like this, that if he had done this against the NRA or Blackwater, George Soros would have bought it for $5 million, and it would be made into a movie that would premiere simultaneously in Westwood, Hollywood, and Cannes, and Laurie David would send her private jet to pick him up and he would end up sitting poolside in Saint-Tropez eating oysters with a little fork while deciding whether or not to return Harvey Weinstein's phone calls.

That wasn't going to happen here. James was exposing a protected Progressive group. The video showed what a "social justice" group actually does behind closed doors with the shakedown money it leeches from the U.S. taxpayers as well as Bank of America and other organizations. The cold, hard reality was that there would be no movie premiere. What he had would be rejected and even derided by ABC News, CBS News, NBC News, and the *New York Times*, and if these amazing videos were to find their way to the American public, it would have to be by a different route.

And this is why I love James. He didn't throw a

tantrum, or blame the messenger. Instead, he believed me, he trusted me. I think he recognized that we shared a common outlook, a desire to loosen the PC stranglehold of the culture through the simple tactic of exposure. Whatever the reason, his nimble mind saw the situation clearly, and jumped immediately to what would be the next step. It was at that moment that my total allegiance to the project really formed, and I realized that we were about to start a long, strange trip together.

Time was wasting—we had to get moving. James had, at this point, four other videos (Washington, DC, New York, Philadelphia, and Baltimore—he was an incredible four-for-four), and we had to get them out there before they leaked and ACORN lawyered up and began devising some bullshit defense. We pledged to work nose to nose to bring the videos out, feeding off of each other's excitement. As James left, I knew I had just had a watershed encounter in my life.

"I want it. I want it I want it I want it I want it I want it," I told Larry. "This is great. This is huge. The media don't want it, but we'll *force* them to watch it." Even Larry agreed. I think I saw his pupils dilate.

What made it all so huge was the unthinkably awful nature of James O'Keefe and Hannah Giles's proposition. I mean, underaged Salvadoran sex slaves? I remember asking Larry if he knew a single person in his life—and we know some pretty depraved people—who would sit there and not bat an eye or look at the person beside them and blurt out, "Are you friggin' kidding me? I'm calling the cops!" What kind of people were these? After all, they weren't just helpful, they were skilled: "social justice" operatives with specialized training to help clients navigate complex governmental assistance programs. These were employees with entrepreneurial know-how and an understanding of the tax code (assuming such an understanding is possible). And they were using all this ability to undermine and exploit the very society that supported them. The footage was so damning, I felt sure that if the American people could see this, it would be impossible for the media to continue rejecting conservatives' cries for investigations of ACORN. I thought the videos could even instigate criminal investigations and inspire whistle-blowers within ACORN itself.

James and Hannah had done their part; now it was up to me to figure out how we would get there from here. How could I get this to the American public? For it was a piece of work both braver and more incisive than whatever twaddle will win the Pulitzers this year.

So over a long night of pacing and cold Chinese

food, we devised a strategy. We understood this was not about a few short-term bucks. This was bigger. There were two targets, essentially: ACORN first, of course, but then the bigger target of a media that would refuse the story. Break the media, and the story breaks.

We also surmised that there was no real exposure to be had on the Internet from a video being seen a million times. The goal couldn't simply be to get as many clicks as possible at Big Government, which would be launched simultaneously with the release of the ACORN videos—that would be a fundamental mistake.[*] I was thinking now with my news aggregator hat on. I knew there was a weird value in nurturing the Internet ecosystem, much more value than there was in simply trying to get people to come to one website to watch one video. In a word, the goal was: ubiquity.

On that basis, the arrangement quickly fell into place. James would be compensated for his work by

---

[*] It's the same mistake any start-up Internet or New Media company makes—to say to the audience, "We want you to come here and we want you to stay here," as though you're the only site on the Internet. With a singular, potentially viral product like a video, the far better strategy is—to quote another famous salesman—"Spread the wealth around."

retaining the rights to it, so that if it hit the stratosphere, he and Hannah would get paid big-time. For my part, I'd be in charge of the rollout, and I would get to launch Big Government with the videos. He'd get the bucks; I'd get the buzz.

For my part, it was a godsend. Big Government was designed to have a limited-government mission, to counter the emerging Obama health-care reform, to stop the expansion of government. The story fit that agenda perfectly. We would create this new website around an emerging, multipart, explosive news item. Big Government would serve as the story's mother ship, seeding what we hoped would be hundreds of news and politics websites simultaneously. For an Internet launch, it was unprecedented.

"You know what, James?" I told him. "We're mutually incentivized to get this story out there." (I actually talk like that.) "If it becomes huge and you own the rights to it, you can make your own documentary. Maybe you guys *will* make some money here. And I don't get anything if I don't help." It was the fairest arrangement I could imagine. All I had to do now was make "those unbelievable ACORN videos" a household phrase.

Luckily, I had a sterling team on board. Big Gov was headed up by a good friend, Mike Flynn (Maura's husband). Aside from being an outstanding writer and editor himself, Mike was by far my number one connector in Washington circles when it came to limited-government and fiscal-responsibility types. His last job had been with the Reason foundation, so his conservative/libertarian credentials were intact. He understood state government because he'd worked there; he understood the federal government as well. He knew the best writers and researchers. So I asked Mike to fly out to California for "an important meeting"; I wanted to do this in person. Sitting across from him, I had only one question that mattered: "What do you know about ACORN?"

A smile broke across his face. "A *lot*."

Mike, it turns out, understood ACORN and its connectivity to the Democratic Party much better than I did—perhaps better than anyone else alive did. He knew that *community organizer* was a pregnant term, stood for a great deal more than most people know, and that we were about to dip our toes into one vast, corrupt ocean.

So we talked. A long time.

Of course, while all this heady momentum was gathering, we were all willfully blind to one little item: Big Government didn't actually *exist* yet. Yes, the pieces were all in place. The concept was honed, the domain name secured, the web interface constructed. But a multitiered news website costs money. Where would we get the scratch to actually create this thing?

The issue could be ignored no longer; we'd been planning Big Government for a long time, and the site would either happen now or it wouldn't. I reached out to one of the only "money" people I knew, told her what we were up to, and told her we needed help. She turned me down flat. She was afraid of the Alinsky playbook, the Richard Mellon Scaife treatment in particular. She has a family, has some public exposure. I couldn't blame her. In her position, who wouldn't be afraid?

It was then I made up my mind. I boldly declared to Larry, "Let's put our money where our mouth is." Larry said, "Okay, but what money?"

Or rather, *Let's put my dad's money where our mouth is*. Yup, I went to Daddy. I told Dad I needed to borrow twenty-five thousand dollars to kick off a website, that it could be a very big thing in my career (whatever that career actually was), and that I would never ask him for anything like it again. He didn't ask questions, God bless him; he just ponied up and wished me luck. I doubt he had any expectations of ever seeing that money again—a *lot* of money, frankly, to a retired restaurateur. But Dad came through. He wasn't afraid. (yes, we've since paid him back.)

And we were rolling.

* * *

The day after James came to my house with the Baltimore video, I took a once-in-a-lifetime week off to be a Lincoln Fellow at the Claremont Institute. It is basically a program where you sit around in a luxury hotel and learn about the Founders from some of the world's best thinkers on American history.

Because of my (somewhat understated) approach to academics during college, I now function in a sort of guilty read-everything mode born of guilt. So the opportunity to be taught about the Founding Fathers by people like Harry Jaffa filled a void left by an American Studies experience at Tulane that had really been a major in anti-American Studies. The Claremont program was fantasy baseball camp for constitutional junkies, and packing to go, I couldn't have been more excited. I did everything but bring a James Madison lunch box.

I checked in to the beautiful Island Hotel in Newport Beach on a warm summer day, feeling like a kid at camp. As soon as I checked in to the room, thinking about the pool and the bar more than Thomas Jefferson just then, I got a call from a guy named Patrick Courrielche. Now, I had just read a piece in *Reason* magazine by Courrielche. Patrick is an artist who started off as a liberal and moved toward libertarianism.[*] His *Reason* piece suggested that his brethren in the art world needed to diversify their ideological holdings, that it was just flat-out boring for everyone to think and create according to the same leftist orthodoxy. Reading his piece, I recognized that at the most basic level, that was my argument about the larger culture, too: *this is boring*. For everybody to have the exact same PC point of view, reinforcing the growth of the state, runs so contrary to what artists should be about—which is challenging conformity. Yet in 2009, conservatives, libertarians, and other rebels found themselves in this ideological ghetto.

For a while after I'd read his piece, Patrick and I had been corresponding. Talking to him now from Claremont, he casually mentioned that he had received an e-mail from the National Endowment for the Arts. It was an invitation to a conference call hosted by the NEA, the White House Office of Public Engagement, and a group called "United We Serve." According to the e-mail, the call was designed to bring together "a group of artists, producers, promoters, organizers, influencers, marketers, taste-makers, leaders, or just plain cool

---

[*]Talk about an apostate to the left—Patrick's former partner is Shepard Fairey, the guy who designed the Obama "Hope" poster.

people to…work together to promote a more civically engaged America and celebrate how the arts can be used for a positive change!" Patrick asked me whether he should tape it. I told him absolutely.

That was because James O'Keefe had already changed my thinking. I had always been a text-based guy—I had founded Breitbart.tv, but that was merely a video aggregator. James had shown me that tape was the most damaging evidence you could have. The conference call took place three days later. And on that conference call, members of the White House staff and the NEA openly asked artists to help promote the Obama agenda.

And Courrielche had it on tape.

If you think about it, the timing was crazy. If you're a conservative and you pay attention to the conservative news cycle, you know that huge stories are relatively rare. And here was a huge story in ACORN, and a pretty big story in the NEA, back-to-back. (Had these been liberal-oriented news items, they would have been presented as somewhere between V-J Day and the moon landing.) Some reporters dine out on a story they did forty years ago, and to put these two stories together at the exact same moment, both of them representing the Democrat-Media Complex's corruption and propagandizing and ends-justify-the-means tactics—it was a breakthrough moment for the New Media. I'm not a religious man, but if anything makes me believe in Divine Providence, it was that convergence.

Because this was the moment. Monica Lewinsky had started it, Swift Boat had continued it by end-running around the media and keeping Kerry out of office, Dan Rather had lost his job, and Clark Hoyt of the *New York Times* would soon admit that the mainstream media were late to the party on Van Jones. But in my mind, it seemed that if the ACORN story and the NEA story could be paired and weaponized, maximized and forced into the eye of the American public, they could serve as a case study demonstrating that the New Media could supplant Ye Olde Media. These paired stories could serve as notice that if the mainstream wouldn't take helpful hints to right the ship, they were going to experience something akin to a mutiny. I felt like Fletcher Christian with an impending case of carpal tunnel.

Incidentally, I was thinking in these grandiose, metaphorically violent terms—in these revolutionary terms, really—because I was simultaneously being taught about the Founding Fathers and the risks that they took and the stakes that were in play during the American Revolution. While the other Lincoln Fellows were sitting there writing notes furi-

ously, like the brilliant academics that they were—
these were the next Newt Gingriches or Antonin
Scalias or Clarence Thomases of the world—I was
sitting there with my New Media mind taking it all
in like it was *Avatar* in 3-D. I started listening to the
stories of the Founding Fathers, the conditions that
they found themselves in, their interactions with
the monarchy and their fellow citizens. I heard that
they were a loose band of malcontents who didn't
have a mass movement behind them.

And I realized that right in front of me—*right in
front of me*—I had the same opportunity, at a critical time in our nation's history, to go against the
grain and to fight a revolution against the Complex. I had a chance to exploit a crack that had
been growing in the mainstream media with the exposure of the Democratic Party–media collusion. I
had a chance to demonstrate that the Complex is
a unitary, tyrannical organism that serves to suffocate those who disagree with its collective worldview
and silly utopian aphorisms.

Call it delusions of grandeur. Call it the "Walking Out of *Rocky* Syndrome," where you shadow-
box the air after you see the film, feeling like a giant
dork but also feeling you can take on the world.
The Claremont Institute inspired me to realize that
I had an obligation to fight the battle against the
oppression and total control of the national air-

waves by the champagne class who seek to build a false and demeaning narrative of what America is and what it should be, who trample on the First Amendment with their Frankfurt School philosophy and Alinsky tactics. The battle against them was a righteous cause. I was certain. And I recognized that by whatever accident of circumstance, I was well-trained and well-positioned for this battle against them, a battle that would take place in the New Media theater of war. And it was my obligation to take up those weapons at my disposal.

I left Claremont prepared for combat. I would need to be.

A Plan took shape.

The release of the Courrielche tape created an online and talkradio sensation and forced the resignation of an NEA appointee. As predicted, the mainstream media did their best to ignore it. It was New Media—including Big Hollywood—that forced the Obama administration to finally do some damage control and take some action. It was an excellent softening up, the "one" in the "one-two" punch we were planning. It did its job.

Now for the haymaker. Of course, I knew the press wasn't going to give credit where it was due on the ACORN story, and that they wouldn't believe that the Plan hadn't all been preconceived. So I took precautions in my *Washington Times* column released September 7, 2009—the Monday before we launched the story.

The piece followed hard on the heels of the Van Jones story. Jones, Obama's appointed "Green Czar," as well as a celebrated communist and "9/11 Truther," had stepped down on September 5 because of conservative media pressure from Glenn Beck, Breitbart.tv, and others. (Beck, by the way, already knew about the ACORN videos at this point—when I showed them to him, he told me, "You need a bodyguard.") Clark Hoyt had written that the *New York Times* had to pay more attention to the conservative media, that the mainstream media had ignored the Van Jones story until it crawled up and bit them on the ass, when Jones was ultimately forced to resign.

Despite that, I *knew* they were going to ignore the ACORN story, too, despite their newfound "commitment" to a wider news angle. So I wrote a column entitled, "Couric Should Look in Mirror." In it, I laid out the entire Plan, getting it into the public record as evidence that I had warned the mainstream media what was coming. In the column, I mentioned the NEA story and I mentioned ACORN. Then I gave them the big clue: "When the next big scandal hits—and it will, and it most certainly won't come from traditional journalism—all eyes will be on 'Pinch' Sulzberger [*New York Times* publisher Arthur O. Sulzberger Jr.] to see if he does his job. All eyes are on the media. We are judging them by the standard they taught us during Watergate: 'The cover-up is worse than the crime.' "[1]

The timing was carefully chosen, and with the backdraft of Jones and Hoyt, sailing conditions were ideal. We launched the week Barack Obama was trying to reset the conversation on health care. This was one month after the violent town hall experiences in which a finger was bitten off in Thousand Oaks by a crazed Obama follower, where a black guy was called the N word and was beaten up by two Service Employees International Union (SEIU) thugs. At this point Obama wanted to reframe the health-care debate, because his original effort had been a muddled failure. Obama was due to make his unprecedented speech to all school-children on Tuesday, September 8; the next day he was set to address a joint session of Congress on health care, all in an attempt to create a fake groundswell where the following conversation would take place between America's kids and their parents:

"Mommy, Mommy! The president spoke. He's so wonderful! Please do whatever it takes to make his presidency a success!"

"Yes, darling. I *shall* support health-care reform, because the day after you heard the president in school, I heard him on television telling me that government-controlled health care is the most important thing in the world, even though every poll shows the American people want jobs and economic recovery rather than a new multi-trillion-dollar entitlement. Hey, isn't that Joy Behar wonderful?"

I had learned from John McCain's choosing Sarah Palin the day after Obama's Invesco Speech—the speech with the Greek columns, the speech that was supposed to announce Obama's godlike ascent to power, one of the "biggest" speeches of all time—that you could suck the air out of the room with a breaking, well-timed story. The day after Invesco, nobody was talking about Invesco—everybody was talking about Palin.

And I knew that for the Obama phenomenon to continue, media control was everything. Here was a construct whom the mainstream covered on a routine basis, whom they never vetted, who was in fact elected by them through platitudes and misdirection. That's why it never crossed my mind whether I should play fair.

Fair loses.

So my goal was to allow Obama to speak on Wednesday night before the joint session of Congress, then drop the first ACORN video early Thursday morning, so that instead of the American public spending the day at the watercooler asking each other, "Did you see the health-care speech? Don't you feel healthier already?" they'd spend the day asking each other, "Holy shit—did you see that ACORN video?" We'd drop the first video Thursday, the second one Friday. I knew also that on Saturday, September 12, the 9/12 Project and the Tea Party movement were planning rallies all over the country, including a massive rally in Washington, DC. So we'd get an early litmus test—in places like Quincy, Illinois, and Washington, DC, we'd be able to see how ordinary Americans were reacting to the scandal.

There was still, however, the question of *which* videos to release. I wanted to launch the Baltimore and Washington tapes in close proximity to each other, so that ACORN and its allies would think these kids had done only a regional hit. It would never occur to them that this story had coast-to-coast implications, that these kids had done something far wider in scope. If I had released the videos from Baltimore and Los Angeles, I figured they would have known the extent of their problem. I also wanted to give them a chance to float the inevitable "a few bad apples" defense. So by making the story regional, I was sandbagging them.

But as we neared launch date, I was worried. We had the what and the when, but the big issue of *where* we should launch still loomed. As much as I wanted to exclusively use the web-based New Media, I wasn't sure I could rely on the ACORN scandal trickling up from just Big Government, YouTube, and the viral Internet. I knew this ground-up strategy might not work, because the Complex had crafted a response to viral stories: Media Matters.

In an effort to act as a firewall to protect the left from ACORN-like stories, and in response to the success of groups like the Swift Boat Vets, the mainstream media had created a rear-protecting unit, Media Matters. Its workers—"senior fellows" as they like to be called—are generally white, web-savvy young guys. Media Matters raises a lot of money, seven to ten million dollars per year, to nitpick a story to death, delegitimizing it, isolating it, and then claiming it has been debunked. The content at Media Matters is then repeated all over the left-wing media, from the networks to MSNBC and CNN to the *New York Times*, as received wisdom.

I knew Media Matters and its ilk could kill off a story before it got started by nitpicking it in its infancy. And let's be honest here, I wasn't dealing from strength; though I had the truth. James O'Keefe and Hannah Giles weren't professional filmmakers. I didn't have a thirty-person staff of reporters or a personal staff or a PR team. So a viral, web-based rollout, however attractive, couldn't be risked. I had to hit overwhelmingly, from all angles. I needed the tsunami. And I needed it to build to the point that it swamped the Media Matters breaching wall and washed right into the newsrooms. Then the mainstream media would have to deal with the fact that they were wet, and the water was rising.

I should mention that as clever or obvious as all this might sound, in retrospect there was no shortage of those who disagreed with me. I had in fact showed the videos to a couple of prominent old-school journalists, and they both told me that the Plan was a loser, that I needed to drop the videos neutron-bomb style—in one place, and all at once. They were also worried about the techniques James and Hannah had used. But talking to them actually strengthened my conviction—their objections sounded musty, outdated; and I realized that on this one I was going to ignore the advice of my elders and betters. I would stick to the "drip-drip-drip from everywhere" strategy I was so convinced would work.

It was time to get started.

I began by giving the Old Guard a fair shot—after all, they were still the prevailing power, and

I couldn't really gripe if they didn't cover a story they hadn't known about. So I approached a contact at ABC News and showed him the videos. He was blown away. But then he told me ABC News would never run it because it was "too political."

I felt vindicated already.

Next, I approached one of my contacts at Fox News. I told him about the ACORN story, and simply handed him a copy of the tapes. I didn't tell him what to do with it. I simply said, "This is what we're going to do on Big Government, and we're going to give you the full audio and video. You can do whatever you want with it. And you can ask James O'Keefe whatever you wish."

Now, I didn't just do this because I wanted the story to break on Fox News (even though I did). I did it because I believed that Roger Ailes and Rupert Murdoch wouldn't launch a story of this magnitude without having the massive legal authority of Fox check to see whether everything was legit. Handing it to Fox News gave me my highest level of confidence. I had a small business running out of a basement—they had a billion-dollar entertainment conglomerate. They were better equipped than I was to ensure that everything was on the straight and narrow. And somewhere in the back of my mind, I still had to worry that maybe I was being punked, and that this was all a giant scheme, that maybe James hadn't told me the whole truth and that I was the target of an even grander plot. Giving the video to Fox News was like enlisting your tough older brother against a pack of schoolyard bullies.

Still, I went to sleep that night with an inkling that something might go wrong. My biggest fear was that Fox would have second thoughts and refuse to launch it, and we'd lose our tsunami. My second-biggest fear—which rose in paranoid moments late in the night—was that Fox would refuse to run it because they had discovered it was a scam and that I was the rube who'd been taken.

At five o'clock in the morning, I got a phone call from my contact at Fox News. "There's a problem," he said. "It was supposed to launch at six with Megyn Kelly. It broke this morning on *Fox & Friends*."

I couldn't even pretend to be upset. Larry and I had been so stressed about launching this story, about having dotted all our *i*'s and crossed all our *t*'s, fearful all the time that something would go seriously wrong—and now I was being told Fox had run with it first thing that morning. It was the equivalent of your wife going into labor two days before the due date, and the doctor apologizing for handing you a perfect baby forty-eight hours early. Our response wasn't angst—it was exultation.

The Fox News call prompted a massive scramble on our part to get all the material up at Big Government right away. Somehow, we did. Fox News was going with it, the print media was teed up, and Big Government was ready. All we could do now was wait.

ACORN itself gave us our first little victory. Scott Levenson, ACORN's spokesman, responded to the regular airing of the Day One video on Fox by claiming that "the portrayal is false.... This film crew tried to pull this sham at other offices and failed." Perfect. So far, everyone was playing their roles (and really, what other defense could Levenson have used?). It worked for us because we knew that Day Two's release, the DC video, would prove that Levenson and the ACORN leadership were either lying or painfully misinformed.

There must have been some panicked strategy sessions and conference calls in the wake of the first video drop, but by the evening of Day One, ACORN made its first attempt at damage control: they fired two of the lackeys in the Baltimore office. "They were two part-time employees," said Baltimore ACORN Co-chairwoman Sonja Merchant-Jones. "One was a receptionist and the other was a part-time tax preparer." To her credit, Merchant-Jones perceived our strategy: "It's no coincidence that this video was released after the president's speech."[2]

She may have understood our timing, but she—

and ACORN itself—clearly thought that would end the story.

Not quite.

On Friday morning, we released the Washington, DC, video. It was just as damning as the Baltimore video. By now, the ACORN tapes were pinging around the Internet, and Fox had the story in steady rotation. We knew that we were drawing blood when ACORN abandoned white spokesperson Scott Levenson in favor of the dashiki-clad African-American Bertha Lewis. Clearly, political correctness, the race card, and Alinsky were going to be their playbook—a tried-and-true defense.

That day, Friday, I flew to Quincy, Illinois, for the 9/12 Tea Party. Right before we got on the airplane, I was informed that ACORN had fired two more employees in DC.

That wasn't a small thing. It meant that we had gotten our *BAM! BAM!* It was a double blow, an affirmation from ACORN that what they were seeing on the video was not only absolutely wrong—it was trouble for them.

I still had the long flight cross-country. I was in the air for four and a half hours, without Internet access, on our way to our stopover in St. Louis. That's my definition of hell, especially at a time when every minute counts (and the in-flight movie stars Ashton Kutcher).

Then I got off the plane. There were twenty-five to thirty people waiting for me at the terminal, all carrying signs about the ACORN scandal. This wasn't my final stop—this was a *stopover*, and they were out there waiting for me to congratulate me. I didn't even know how they'd found me, or what I was being congratulated for. Then somebody told me: the Census had de-linked from ACORN. Census Bureau director Robert Groves wrote a letter to ACORN in which he explained that "recent events concerning several local offices of ACORN have added to the worsening negative perceptions of ACORN and its affiliation with our partnership efforts." Census Bureau spokesman Stephen Buckner told the press, "Their affiliation caused sufficient concern with the general public [that their continued participation would be] a distraction from our mission, and would maybe even be a discouragement" to Americans participating.[3]

When we finally got to Quincy and the Tea Party itself, the crowd was raucous. At least a third of the signs were targeting ACORN. The story was exploding.

It was clear that this wasn't just an A story, this was an A+ story—ACORN's reaction had guaranteed us that. The political class was noticing the story, and the mainstream media could pretend not to notice, but the water was already up to their waists.

When I listened to my voice mail, there was one from Sean Hannity. "Andrew," he said, "you need to come up to New York."

I whispered to myself, "Wow. This thing just jumped another notch."

For media types, despite all the talk of decentralizing the news business (including my own), the island of Manhattan remains the promised land. The major networks, Fox News, the other cable news outlets, the major newsmagazines—all remain cloistered together in this leftie hothouse dedicated to one-upmanship. Baltimore and DC are big towns, but the world pays attention to what happens in Manhattan, and for the ACORN story to truly hit the stratosphere—to truly swamp Ye Olde Media—we would have to flood the Big Apple.

Bertha Lewis certainly helped. She responded to the Day Two drop by claiming that Hannah and James had been kicked out of ACORN's Los Angeles, Philadelphia, and New York offices. "This recent scam, which was attempted in San Diego, Los Angeles, Miami, New York, Philadelphia, to name a few places, had failed for months before the results we've all recently seen," she responded on Fox. This was, quite simply, a lie, and now, with videos from all those locations in hand, we knew we had them. It was time to take this road show to Broadway.

Lewis teed up the New York City video better than I could have imagined. With a pimp-and-prostitute photo in hand disproving her assertion that the New York ACORN office had resisted James's pitch, I made a call to a top executive at the *New York Post*. By this point, the story was really gaining momentum, and I was feeling confident if I offered the print exclusive to the *Post*, they'd run the story the following Monday morning. They did it. And so for two days, Monday and Tuesday, Hannah and James were plastered on the front page in newsstands across New York City, the stories inarguably disproving every defense ACORN was mustering. Talk about assaulting the Old Media: the story was now simply unavoidable. The smile on my face, hunkered in my secret Manhattan hotel like some New Media seditionist, was from knowing that even in their townhouses and limousines, Pinch Sulzberger and Jonathan Klein and Katie Couric could ignore this no longer.

While in retrospect the ACORN rollout appears — even to me — seamlessly choreographed and executed, in actuality it was two of the craziest weeks of my life. If any of us got more than three hours of sleep any night, I'd be surprised. It was all a roller-coaster blur of travel, phone calls, e-mails, offers, pitches, and threats. The phone would ring, you'd answer it, and suddenly the story—and our lives— would keep accelerating. We held it together because we believed in what we were doing, believed that the people we were exposing were the tip of the corrupt, venal, leftist spear for whom America was nothing more than a deserving victim. We also held it together because we had a special team.

While I had already met James, I actually met Hannah Giles for the first time in New York. All three of us—James, Hannah, and I—were staying at the same hotel in different rooms. I could tell right away that we were going to get along. She was ebullient, a trouper to beat all troupers. She was immediately my friend and my fellow warrior, and even though twenty years separated us, I said to myself, *I think this person understands what is going on here and can handle it.*

James was in a different boat. While we were blood brothers because of the story, James was a creative genius—but also a mess. He had to edit all the videos for release, often to different specifications for different news outlets, so if I was sleep-deprived during all this, James was a full-on zombie. As we pressed on all fronts, I was actually worried about his health.

Hannah started going on TV and started to win over the audience. That was an X-factor we hadn't planned on; that the beautiful young woman playing a prostitute in the videos would come across as so poised, grounded, and mature on television. The first time Larry and I saw Hannah appearing on the *Glenn Beck* show, we turned to each other and said, "This is masterful." Hannah played it all so well, letting the videos tell the story, driving home the key points with pithy phrases. This wasn't a snotty kid playing "Gotcha!" Here was a serious young woman who understood what she was doing, and what was more: *she wasn't afraid.*

As for James: Apparently he had been burned before by partners who got lots of media attention. He had collaborated with other conservatives, and they had often gotten the credit, and I knew that he wanted this story to be the beginning of his career and his notoriety in the same way I wanted to be recognized for my understanding of how the media work. And I wanted it for him. He deserved it.

That was why I knew I had to manage the story down to its most minute detail. It really was an extraordinary accomplishment to get James to understand that he had to give me full transcripts and audio so that we could do due diligence, to ensure that everything was aligned and in sequence. I had to win his trust, and despite his youth James was quite cynical on that score. Ultimately, James agreed to it, but it ran contrary to what he had done in the past. I told James I'd ensure he got the full credit he was due, but I also told him they were going to hold us to standards to which they don't hold *60 Minutes* or *Dateline NBC*. He had to give up some control—so that I could trust him as well.

So when the story broke, while I was on television translating for the public Mike Flynn's expertise in the Democratic machine's relationship with corrupt "community organizers," James was hunched over a computer in a cluttered hotel room preparing the video that would support that analysis. Neither piece worked nearly as well without the other, and none of it worked unless we totally trusted each other. It was a bond formed in the media war trenches. This side of Afghanistan, you can't get tighter than that.

On Monday morning, we released the New York ACORN video.

Our world detonated.

As I previously mentioned, we had worked over the weekend with the *New York Post* to give them the print exclusive on the New York video. We felt that the third video was going to be the charm, because once people realized there was a third video, they'd think there was a fourth, a fifth, a sixth, a hundredth. The fact that the third video was New York—and the fact that the *Post* put a lurid shot of James and Hannah on the cover in their pimp and prostitute outfits—just opened the floodgates. That day, the Brooklyn DA's office said they would investigate ACORN for possible criminality. It was everywhere, and as the talk of criminal charges surfaced, the mainstreamers could no longer afford to ignore it. This story just wouldn't be confined to regional newspapers and talk radio. It was national. The only question was who in the Old Media would be the first to crack.

The next day, we did it again. We released the Riverside, California, video, in which Tresa Kaelke tried to help James and Hannah, and told a story about how she had murdered an ex-husband. Kaelke encouraged them to set up the brothel, offering to help. And again, it made the cover of the *New York Post*. Two days, two walk-off homers.

That day, Congress voted to defund ACORN. It wasn't even close—the House voted 345–75, and the Senate voted 85–11 to end ACORN's cash flow. The Democrats largely did it to cover their asses, but at least one Democrat seemed truly upset. "I am outraged at the actions of ACORN's employees and believe they should be penalized to the full extent of the law," said Rep. Zack Space (D-OH). "Our government must be vigilant in ensuring that organizations that are found to act fraudulently do not receive taxpayer dollars."[4]

That same day, the media reported that Bill Clinton had gotten together over lunch with Barack Obama. These two are not friends. It was Clinton who suggested to Ted Kennedy that Kennedy had endorsed Obama "because he's black." It was Clinton who told Kennedy that "a few years ago this guy would have been getting us coffee." Now he was sitting across the table from Obama—supposedly discussing health care.

Now, why would Obama discuss health care with the guy who had failed to get health care passed in the early days of his presidency?

I firmly believe that Obama wasn't there to discuss health care. Here we were, six days after Obama's "reset" on health care before the joint session of Congress, and the ACORN scandal was on the cover of the *Post*. It was on TV. It was everywhere. We had released four videos. By Tuesday, Obama clearly was paying attention to the fact that his organization was under siege. He was aware of the fact that his Complex was lying every step of the way and getting nailed in the lies; he was aware of the fact that the media—*his* media—were getting nailed when they accepted Bertha Lewis and ACORN's ludicrous excuses. How many more days could new video come out, and the press provide cover for them? Obama knew it had to end.

That was why Clinton was there. It was a sign that Obama was facing a potential Lewinsky scandal. He understood that things were spiraling out of control. He needed a strategy—and that was where Clinton came in. Perhaps I'm being a bit hubristic, but I'm convinced that this was the meeting in which Obama and Clinton decided to put John Podesta in charge of the ACORN response team. The truth is that Obama didn't have much choice. The Tea Parties were gaining credence and weight, the main topic of the Tea Parties was ACORN, and the dam was about to burst.

That night, it finally did. Both Katie Couric and Jon Stewart broke the mainstream media embargo on the story. Stewart's story was particularly huge, because if you're ACORN and you've lost Jon Stewart, you've lost everything. When I saw that Stewart had bashed ACORN, I said to Hannah and James, "You know how I've been fretting and worrying at every stage? I think you guys are out of harm's way now."

The Obama team began to respond in earnest the next day with tried-and-true Clintonian tactics. ACORN announced its "independent" investigation panel. The members? Podesta himself, SEIU president Andy Stern, and former Housing and Urban Development secretary Henry Cisneros (investigated plenty of times in his own right). Head-ing up the team: former Massachusetts attorney general Scott Harshbarger, who had pushed the false prosecution of Gerald Amirault back during his district attorney days.[*] It was a team designed to obfuscate, not investigate. There was no way I was going to cooperate with these hacks.

As the whitewash began, we showed we weren't done, either. On Wednesday, we released the San

---

[*]The *Wall Street Journal* summed up Harshbarger's behavior in that infamous case when Amirault was released after nearly two decades in prison: "Along the way, the law was stood on its head. The rules of evidence were changed to accommodate the prosecution; the burden of proof was put on the accused. Four- and five-year-olds were coached to say what adults wanted to hear. One of the reasons behind the district attorney's decision last week not to oppose Mr. Amirault's release on parole was that in order to have him classified as a 'sexually dangerous person' there would have had to be a virtual retrial of the entire Amirault case. The DA had to have been deterred by the prospect of parading into a courtroom with the incredible fantasies extracted from Mr. Amirault's alleged victims—about secret rooms, magic drinks, animal butchery, assaults by a bad clown. Then District Attorney Scott Harshbarger had offered them as 'proof' of the Amiraults' guilt."

Diego videos, which again showed an ACORN employee helping James and Hannah set up an underage brothel at taxpayer expense.

But we had a problem on Thursday. We didn't know what to do next. The Plan had gone so well, it had run its course faster than expected. *Now what?* I thought. *Should we keep releasing videos?* We still had several more—in fact, as of this writing, we still do—but we didn't want to run out.

That was when Baltimore's ACORN told us they were going to sue us.

I still can't believe they filed a complaint just then. It served our ends perfectly, because I wanted to create the perception that there were unlimited videos, but we were running out. Now, I've been in a lawsuit before. It's not a pleasant experience. But this one put a smile on my face, because the idea that I would get into discovery with ACORN—and the knowledge that I was in the legally and morally righteous position—was awesome. I would hire the best Federalist Society lawyers in the world to dig through ACORN's muck. When they sued me, I actually responded out loud: "It's Christmas." All their lawsuit did was intertwine me in the mythology of ACORN. All my dreams and aspirations for getting into high-level intrigue were starting to materialize. I was enjoying it so much that it felt like I was simultaneously on every single class-A narcotic that has ever been banned. I felt that I shouldn't be allowed to drive, I was so giddy with what was happening.

Meanwhile, I merrily tweaked with the media's heads. They had been coming to me throughout the entire rollout. I knew that the media were a natural conduit to the other side, sort of like discovery for ACORN in a high-stakes lawsuit. ACORN and the Obama administration and their media allies weren't going to be giving us information about their strategy, I knew, so why should I give them the information they could use to attempt to outplay us? We knew that the press was there to play defense for Obama, and we knew that in many cases, reporters and publishers were attempting to grill me for information so that they could craft their revised playbook.

So we screwed around with them. And I told them we were playing with them. When Carol Leonnig of the *Washington Post* asked me how many videos there were, I told her I wouldn't tell her. She asked why, and I told her: "I'm screwing with you."

It was an entertaining and illuminating interview, to say the least. She asked me what I felt when I saw the videos. "When I saw the first one," I replied, "I thought it was an anomaly. When I saw the second one, I thought it was a coincidence. When I saw the third one, I knew it was a trend.

When I saw these videos, I couldn't help thinking, 'This is the Abu Ghraib of the Great Society.' "

That got her goat. She got viscerally upset. She told me she was part of the *Washington Post* team that had won awards for its coverage of Abu Ghraib.

"Do you really want to have an argument over this?" I asked her. "That was one National Guard unit that the press used to hang as an albatross around the Bush administration, to make it a symbol of its wartime policy, to extrapolate that its waterboarding policy and interrogation policy were tied to a widespread anti-Muslim humiliation campaign. The National Guard unit was sufficiently punished and there was a straightforward investigation. There was no attempt to cover it up. It was a clean bust and it was a clean cleanup, but it was hardly representative of a massive trend."

She told me why she thought I was wrong, and why this wasn't anything like Abu Ghraib. "You just caught a bunch of dummies on video!" she said.

The irony was both painful and delicious. "That's what Bush called the 'soft bigotry of lowered expectations,' " I noted. "Those people were smart enough to rig the system to defraud taxpayers." That much was obvious, after all. So while Leonnig saw a bunch of low-income, mostly minority community organizers as dummies, duped by predatory Repugnicans, to everyone who actually watched the videos it was clear these were well-trained and well-informed operators, committed to navigating an intricate web of government and private services in order to suckle at the government teat.

The conversation summed up everything that was wrong with the mainstream media. They think it's their obligation to take down right-of-center organizations; they feel it's their raison d'être to attack conservative institutions mercilessly. But if I did the same with a liberal institution, I was victimizing an isolated "bunch of dummies."

ACORN proved that we didn't have to live with their old standards anymore. We could take down the Complex on our own, and we could use the media — could shame the media — into helping. As Jon Stewart, as dependable a media foot soldier as the Dems have, put it after airing the videos on his show: "Are you fucking kidding me?! Investigative media . . . you're telling me that two kids from the cast of *High School Musical 3* can break this story with a video camera and their grandmother's chinchilla coat, and you got nothing?"

The next six months played out absurdly by plan. It's one thing to have theories about the Complex, but it's quite another to put those theories into practice, to see the components falling into place based upon your understanding of the other side. We knew they'd ignore and deny, so we planted the videos one at a time. We knew that as time went on, the media would have to pick it up, expediting ACORN's downfall. And we knew that they could malign James, Hannah, and me as much as they wanted—and that it wouldn't work, because seeing was believing.

Only five months later could the Podesta team try their typical tactic of going after irrelevant details of the story—"Was O'Keefe wearing the outlandish pimp costume?" But by then, it was far too late to try shifting the focus to such ancillary details. ACORN was done. The game was over.

The biggest key to the success of the ACORN story was the structure we had created. I am a single organism who can act swiftly and make decisions on the fly. The Complex is a leviathan, an entity that moves slowly, that has natural momentum and can't stop on a dime. The Democratic Party, Barack Obama, the Progressive movement, John Podesta, and George Soros—all these entities have to *coordinate* their counterstrategy, create a game plan. I don't have that problem. I can stick and move. And I know them down to their core. I understand their Alinsky mind-set, their Clinton mind-set, their Podesta mind-set, their Media Matters mind-set. They are *entirely predictable*. People who grant me expertise in media tactics don't seem to recognize how ordinary the Complex's reactions were. Every step of the way

I predicted how they were going to behave, and every step of the way they came through.

Even now, it continues. John Podesta and Media Matters keep making the same mistakes, which seem to be granting me benefits that weren't originally taken into account at the beginning. The more they come after us—and they do, with every challenging story we publish—the bigger we get. And the bigger we get, the more opportunities we're getting to do other stories, to work with other people who work with us. As they try to destroy us, they are Palin-izing us, making us larger and stronger.

ACORN could have stopped this at the very beginning. They could have acknowledged systemic failure, hired somebody who would have done an honest and thorough investigation and come up with harsh conclusions. They could have engaged in a Nixonian "modified limited hangout."* But I was betting that they were so unused to being challenged, so inherently arrogant, that they wouldn't. They were so sure that their media allies would help them that they fought us every step of the way, and every step of the way emboldened us.

On February 22, 2010, Politico.com reported

---

*Never heard the term? No, it's not an exotic cocktail served at the Watergate Hotel bar. You'll have to Google it, I'm afraid.

that ACORN had "dissolved as a national structure." On March 23, 2010, Reuters reported that ACORN would be formally disbanding due to monetary problems.

On April 1, 2010, the House Committee on Oversight and Government Reform's ranking member, Darrell Issa (R-CA), released a report finding that ACORN "is attempting to rebrand itself without instituting real reforms or removing senior leadership figures that need to be held accountable for wrongdoing. These newly renamed organizations are like career criminals who adopt aliases without changing their criminal lifestyles."[5]

It's not over yet. We remain vigilant to expose the corruption. Because we proved it. We—you and I—can beat them.

CHAPTER 9

Tea Party Protector

On April 15, 2009, I was invited to my first Tea Party in Santa Ana, California. I dragged along my friend, actor Gary Graham, and my father-in-law, Orson Bean. We met Ian Mitchell, the newly naturalized American citizen from the '70s Scottish music sensation the Bay City Rollers (yes, that Bay City Rollers). We met hundreds of the nicest, most congenial, most pro-America people you'd ever want to meet. Blacks and Hispanics and whites, and a labradoodle dressed in a red, white, and blue sweater.

Everyone talked about the Founding Fathers and the Constitution and the Declaration of Independence, about conservative principles. It was like the Claremont Institute, but with everyday working people. And labradoodles.

I was slated to speak at the event. At first, I walked

around the arena's perimeter, observing, taking it all in. But enough people had seen me on TV and the web by now that many approached me to chat. It was a great experience, exciting and affirming. It's actually fun to be around people who *like* you (I'm not used to that in my neighborhood these days). I suspect, however, that for many Tea Partiers, I was a bit of a broken record. Because I was by now fixated on a single topic: what was about to happen to them.

While everyone else talked about what the Tea Party stood for—limited government, lower taxes, less spending—I was compelled to talk about what it would take to protect this movement. I told everyone I could that they had started an uprising, and that the Obama administration and the media wouldn't stand for it. I said that they'd be labeled racists and hatemongers and violent criminals, that they'd be depicted as the dregs of society, people to be excluded from dinner parties because of their made-up closet KKK status. They were about to be targeted, and I knew it. I had to warn them.

I was right, of course. It took the Complex awhile to catch on, but once they did...

After ACORN, the bull's-eye on the Tea Party movement had only seemed to grow. The Tea Partiers were attuned to the ACORN scandal from the get-go—anti-ACORN placards were immediately a fixture at the movement's gatherings following the videos' releases. ACORN was a perfect foil for a movement founded on rejecting covert and overt government corruption and the lack of oversight on federal money distribution. There was no way that could be tolerated for long.

At the same time, however, and despite the media's best efforts, ACORN had grown to embody a hell of a lot more than ACORN itself. The scandal started to expose the political Complex in a dramatic way, the same way we were hoping to expose the cultural Complex with Big Hollywood. Suddenly, people began to see where all the leftist parts fit together: Andy Stern and the SEIU; Obama and Rahm Emanuel and the other White House thugs; ACORN and its on-the-ground fraud; Media Matters and its consistent attempts to keep the media in line, doing the bidding of one side while attempting to shut down the other. Like 1950s America gradually waking up to the existence of the mafia, more and more people were beginning to see the Complex. And this further fed the Tea Party movement, vindicated them, let them know that they weren't seeing phantoms or descending into paranoia. They truly *were* getting screwed.

And ACORN showed them they could fight back.

Because of my self-adopted role of becoming the

Tea Party's protector from the media, I started to become a fixture, the guy who would playbook the offense/defense scheme we needed to counter the inevitable Complex crackdown. "This is the media, and this is what they're going to do to you," I told them every chance I got. "You're focusing on what the country needs to do, and I'm telling you that you need to focus on the key to the whole ball game—the media." Because more than anyone, I knew what these people—little old ladies and retired veterans and young libertarians who hadn't even known they were libertarians until Obama—I knew what they were up against. And it wasn't going to be pretty.

It got ugly fast enough. The Tea Party had been shortchanged for over a year already, with CNN's Anderson Cooper and MSNBC's Keith Olbermann and Rachel Maddow labeling them "tea baggers" and claiming that they were holdover refugees from *Birth of a Nation*. Even for me, it was stunning how the press was willing to attack head-on hundreds of thousands of people exercising their constitutional rights to free speech and freedom of association. Senate Majority Whip Dick Durbin (D-IL) picked up on the cue and demonstrated true statesmanship by himself using the egregious term "tea baggers." House Speaker Nancy Pelosi (D-CA) went pure Alinsky and told the media that protesters were carrying "swastikas and symbols like that."[1] The Hollywood contingent wouldn't be outdone, of course, with Janeane Garofalo calling Tea Partiers "racist rednecks who hate blacks," while Nobel Prize–winning economist Paul Krugman wrote in the *New York Times* that they were driven by "cultural and racial fear."

Then, a new low. In August 2009, MSNBC took a photo of a man carrying a gun at a rally, but cut off his head and hands in the photo, as Contessa Brewer intoned, "There are questions about whether this has racial overtones…white people showing up with guns." Dylan Ratigan and Toure agreed with her. There was only one problem: the guy carrying the gun was *black*. MSNBC had deliberately cropped the picture to try to avoid the inconvenient fact that it contradicted their (false) narrative. They were making it up, using Photoshop to propagate a lie. Where was Media Matters now?

At the same time, SEIU gangsters in St. Louis were beating up a black man, Kenneth Gladney, and calling him the N word for handing out "Don't Tread on Me" flags at a town hall meeting for Rep. Russ Carnahan (D-MO). In Thousand Oaks, California, a liberal activist confronted a Tea Party guy and *bit his finger off*. Yet the media ignored these incidents and instead tried to find the smoking gun of racism that just *had* to be hidden in the Tea Party DNA.

But they couldn't find anything.

So they manufactured it. As the health-care debate drew to a close, the Democratic Party turned to its new primary concern: destroying the uprising.

The first sign that a plan was in place was the ham-fisted, high-camp posturing of the congressional Black Caucus to walk through the peaceful Tea Party demonstrators on their way to vote for the health-care bill on March 20, 2010. There was no reason for these elected officials to walk above-ground through the media circus. The natural route is the tunnels between the House office buildings and the Capitol. By crafting a walk of the Congressional Black Caucus through the crowd, the Democratic Party was looking to provoke a negative reaction. They didn't get it. So they lied about it.

They claimed immediately, without any proof, that black congressmen had been spit at and slurred with the N word fifteen times (as Indiana representative André Carson stated and the press dutifully reported). Soon thereafter Nancy Pelosi walked through this alleged hate-fest with a gavel in hand and that marionette grin affixed to her face. Had the incidents reported by the Congressional Black Caucus actually occurred, the Capitol Police would never have allowed the least popular person in Congress (to that crowd, anyway) to walk right into harm's way.

To reiterate: there was *no proof* that the N word was used, or that anyone was purposefully spit upon. That Tea Party crowd was a sea of New Media equipment. Not only were hundreds of people armed with Handycams, BlackBerrys, and iPods, so were the mainstream media, which had come in expectation of a display of violence and backwardness by the Neanderthal Tea Partiers. They were there, covering every inch of the event. Does anyone really think that somehow they just missed it?

But never mind producing proof themselves. Let's ask another question. Why didn't a single mainstream media outlet even *suggest* that a video should exist to prove these events occurred? This was the same press that was still telling me that we hadn't proved that ACORN was aiding and abetting illegal activity, that our videos were somehow faulty or edited or falsified. "Truth to power," indeed.

The strategy adopted by Nancy Pelosi on health care soon made it clear why it was so important that these charges go unchallenged: race would be the centerpiece of her strategy to destroy the Tea Party movement. She quickly linked the health-care bill to the Civil Rights Act, and her media followers parroted her. The implication: if you were against health care, you hated black people—specifically, President Obama. Throw in the manufactured "N word" strategy and you have a devious scheme designed to take down the Tea Party.

The Democratic Party and the media simply never tire of this approach. It hadn't worked when Bertha Lewis defended ACORN, because we'd had videotapes. Here, without video, the Dems were free to conjure racism from thin air. Suddenly, every liberal outlet in the country—which is to say, virtually every outlet in the country—was simultaneously arguing that the Tea Party was racist and violent, a divisive and irresponsible contention lacking any shred of supporting evidence, except for the observation that the majority of the Tea Partiers were white. Well, so is the country. This was Duke Lacrosse politics at its worst.

The press went directly to petrified Republican leaders, who offered the predictable fearful apologies they weren't qualified to give. I was becoming more Tea Party than GOP every day.

It was all a setup, and I knew it. I smelled a rat. Time to hone my media chops again.

Five days after the highly publicized incidents supposedly happened, I publicly offered ten thousand dollars to anyone for any evidence of use of the N word at the March 20 Tea Party rally. I wrote:

If we let them get away with Saturday's stunt— using the imagery of the Civil Rights era and hurtful lies to cast aspersions upon the Tea Party whole—then they really will have won the day. It's time for the allegedly pristine character of Rep. John Lewis to put up or shut up. Therefore, I am offering $10,000 of my own money to provide hard evidence that the N-word was hurled at him not 15 times, as his colleague reported, but just once. Surely one of those two cameras wielded by members of his entourage will prove his point. And surely if those cameras did not capture such abhorrence, then someone from the mainstream media—those who printed and broadcast his assertions without any reasonable questioning or investigation—must themselves surely have it on camera. Of course we already know they don't. If they did, you'd have seen it by now. THOUSANDS OF TIMES. Rep. Lewis, if you can't do that, I'll give him a backup plan: a lie detector test. *If* you provide verifiable video evidence showing that a single racist epithet was hurled as you walked among the Tea Partiers, or you pass a simple lie detector test, I will provide a $10K check to the United Negro College Fund.[2]

There was not one response.

Predictably, we were five full news days into this

major controversy and there was still no evidence
of such outrageous charges. In fact, the existing
footage from that day showed members of the CBC
walking through the crowd, never once moving
their heads in reaction to any outbursts. Is it con-
ceivable that *all* of them stoically walked by as the
N word was hurled at them fifteen times—even
as the media were holding up cameras, practically
begging the crowd to do something awful?

After my offer was mentioned on both *The Sean
Hannity Show* and *The O'Reilly Factor*, I raised my
offer to twenty thousand dollars. A few days later,
at the Tea Party in Searchlight, Nevada, I upped
the ante to one hundred thousand dollars. As of
November 2010, nobody has stepped forward to
claim the money. When Ken Vogel of Politico.com
covered my offer, he said that calls to Rep. John
Lewis weren't returned.

We called their bluff. And for several weeks, they
tried to back off it. They even refused to answer
any questions about it. Then they tried the usual
Media Matters tactic of attacking an ancillary issue
and trying to discredit the whole story with it. This
time, the contention was that when I posted video
from the March 20 rallies of Lewis and Co. walking
through the crowd, the video was of them walking
away from—not to—the Capitol. Well, here's my
considered response: Who cares? I can't prove a

negative with any videos I create—it's up to *them* to prove their allegations. They haven't done it and they won't do it, because what they claim happened *never happened*.

We even found four videos from the exact place and time showing Representatives Carson and Lewis walking briskly and unobstructed. Four videos. Four angles. No N word. And even then the congressmen and the media refused to take it back. It was an epic victory for truth and absolute proof that the media are the problem.

But what if I hadn't offered the reward, or shown the four videos, and called them on it? How many more times would the left invoke these fake "racism" charges? Do they never learn? It failed with the Duke University lacrosse team; as it did with Professor Madonna Constantine and her faked noose incident at Columbia University (in which Constantine, under investigation by the university for plagiarism, attempted to misdirect and manufacture a hate crime by placing a noose on her own door); as it did with the Sergeant Crowley boner by Barack Obama, who reflexively suggested that a white police officer had behaved "stupidly." The first Alinsky president was using surrogates in the press and in the Congress to split this nation into two hostile parties so he could puppeteer the Have-Nots against the perceived Haves. The silence over the hundred-thousand-dollar challenge, though, was a tacit acknowledgment that the Congressional Black Caucus and Barack Obama don't have the stomach for doubling down. They got caught, pure and simple. But they'll try it again. Which is when they *must* be challenged. Again.

The other half of the strategy that was built into the N-Word Capitol Hill Walk was the desire to incite an overreaction, or even violence. The media did their part by labeling and slandering the Tea Partiers as racist knuckle-draggers, of course (MSNBC's Rachel Maddow referred to the Tea Partiers' missing "white hoods"). Absent any evidence other than creatively selected, handcrafted signs from the fringe of the audience that were taken to represent the whole, Reid and Pelosi's media hand puppets regurgitated the Obama opinion that everyone who doesn't agree with the One is a bitter clinger who relies on God, guns, and racism to get through his or her humdrum little life out in flyover country. This was hardcore media elitism mixed with politically correct class warfare. Pure Alinsky.

Don't believe me? Think I'm a tad paranoid? A little story for you.

The events at the Searchlight, Nevada, Tea Party on March 27, 2010, is the Rosetta Stone of the Democratic Party strategy—a key to understanding how they operate in the trenches. Searchlight is Harry Reid's hometown, and in March of 2010 Sarah Palin and the Tea Party Express rolled into town on the beginning of their cross-country tour. I was invited to speak, and a team of fellow Tea Partiers were actually following me around to film the whole event. Now, none of us were going to Senator Harry Reid's office building to threaten individuals that March day—Harry doesn't even have an office there. We went that day to the middle of the desert to talk up the Constitution and founding documents, and to express our dismay with the current political class. The real astroturf, the bought-and-paid-for union support network that does the heavy lifting and the bone breaking, traveled to Searchlight for one reason: a fight.

Now, I'm by nature a pretty garrulous and easygoing guy, and I don't look for a fight. But somehow, since ACORN, the fight seemed to find me. That was the way it happened on the way to Searchlight. As part of the Express wagon train, I was driving my car from Laughlin to Searchlight, which is truly in the middle of nowhere. As we entered town I saw some of the camera crew, who were ahead of me in the caravan, in a parking lot. They directed me into the lot, and I parked there—I thought we were going to walk to the main event from here. What the hell did I know? Like I've been to Searchlight before?

Getting out of the car, I saw that among the crowds beginning to fill the area up were approximately fifty Harry Reid supporters holding up various union-printed placards. As it began to dawn on me that I might not be where I was supposed to be, I spotted a man who looked liked *Children of the Corn* meets *River's Edge* holding up a sign that read "SEARCHLIGHT →." Problem was, it seemed to be pointing *away* from where I thought we were headed. When I approached him and asked him about it, he told me with a leer that he was directing Tea Party people down the wrong road.

"Now why would you do that?" I asked him.

That's when things started to go south. As if they'd received a psychic signal from this astroturf rabble-rouser in front of me, the entire group of Reid supporters suddenly thronged me, a few shouting, "Hey, I've seen you on TV! I've seen you on MSNBC on Dylan Ratigan's show!" Uh-oh.

As this happened, a Tea Party Express bus drove past. Distracted from me for the moment, some of the crowd started flinging eggs against the side of the bus. As I realized this had been what they were waiting for all along, I yelled, "What are you doing? Who did that?" The crowd began to push the perpetrators away, then created a wall of people to obscure the egg throwers from our cameras (yes, the crew was rolling tape). Protecting its own, the group suddenly became even nastier, and rather—animated.

Luckily, the cameras were still rolling, protecting me against false charges (and against violent activity, because who wants to be videoed pounding on an unarmed Tea Partier?), so I wasn't fearful. Then the Reid supporters tried to block the cameras by holding up their signs.

Now, I don't like backing down from a confrontation, but there were some intensely threatening people there. People were calling me every name you can think of (and some you probably can't). One kept screaming, "Get out of here, rich guy!" (This at a time I still owed my dad that $25K.) And naturally, the race card came right out, with a black guy calling me (how original!) a racist. As gently as I could and still be heard amid that crowd, I told him, "Name one thing I've ever said that's racist." His face simply contorted in rage. That's when I heard another guy scream close to my ear, "I'm going to have to go to jail today if we don't get this guy out of here." The cameras were blocked; I was surrounded. Now I *was* getting scared.

So I got out of there. As I backed toward my car, a group of police officers drove up. Saved! Then one of the cops leaned out the window of his SUV and called out to me. "You need to come over here."

"Yes, Officer," I answered.

"Why were you over there?"

I told him what had happened. He then told me that the Reid supporters had called the police *on me*. "That group of people said you threw eggs and instigated what just happened," he said.

I said, "Excuse me?! I have a camera guy with me, and you can see what happened on the video."

The cops saw their local union pals had picked the wrong target—end of police encounter. But still, the officers didn't go after their local union pals.

Now, the Democratic Party has accused every Tea Party of being astroturfed—of "flying in" agitators to pose as grassroots locals. They accuse the Tea Parties of being propagated by the Republican Party, by white supremacist groups, by a secret cabal of neocon industrialists. But what I had just experienced was astroturfing at its worst—outside agitators from God knows where dropped in to intimidate and harass a peaceful, legal gathering. It was reminiscent of 1930s-style labor coercion.

I had written about these types of tactics and I knew they had happened, but to experience it—to look into the eyes of these people and try to reason with them and realize the uselessness of it—was a revelation. These people were simply looking for trouble and would not take no for an answer. They were there to be a problem. Period.

After reviewing the tape, we were able to identify one of the main culprits in the crowd: Brian DiMarzio, who in fact can be seen clearly on the tape blaming me to the cops (though the video clearly shows otherwise). Who is Brian, you ask? The field director for the Nevada Democratic Party.

Naturally, the usual Podesta/Media Matters apologists leaped to diminish the encounter (which was fairly widely reported). Media Matters "Senior Fellow" Eric Boehlert called my oral and written reports about the event "the Phantom Egg," calling into question my truthfulness.

But of course—thank you, James!—I had the video. It showed clearly that Harry Reid's little foot soldiers were not only there to misdirect traffic, they had also thrown the eggs and called the police. What childishness—what low-rent, schoolyard nonsense. And it might have worked—I might easily have been arrested, and you can imagine how that would have played in the press. But in this age of New Media, the tape (or, as with the N-word accusations, the lack thereof) usually tells the tale. I once again released the video to the media, and even Jon Stewart, who regularly mocks the Tea Partiers, was appalled. After he rolled the video we shot (which clearly depicted one of Reid's supporters holding an egg) on his show, Stewart shouted to the camera: "You're not helping!"

It is they who are violent, not we. They called us racists and couldn't deliver the goods. They called us violent and couldn't deliver the goods. Now they're even trying to infiltrate the Tea Parties and plant violent, psychopathic liberals and union thugs who want to make the Tea Partiers look bad—and they *still* won't be able to deliver the goods.

They need to marginalize and demonize those that would stand up to their hardball, toxic, antidemocratic tactics. That's why they had Bill Clinton out front and center, saying that the Tea Party rhetoric is the same kind of rhetoric that drove Timothy McVeigh to commit his evil acts. That's why Obama is outright dismissive of the Tea Parties—he thinks the usual tactics will work. He literally laughs them off, the epitome of smug arrogance.

But it won't work. Given a fair hearing, given just the slightest bit of exposure—and the American people will rise to the occasion. They see these tactics for what they are.

Will the media keep falling into the trap of blind support of this agenda? Of condescending to and misleading the American people? After all, the current media business model takes another hit each and every time they get suckered into this stuff. Unless they care more about politics than money-making—and if they do, that puts the lie to their argument that they're just profit-seeking enterprises rather than branches of the Democratic Party—it makes no sense. Are they more deeply wedded to their Complex mind-sets than their own solvency? It looks like the answer is yes, as Keith Olbermann's liberal-leaning audience buys into everything he says, Rachel Maddow alienates everyone but the converted, CNN implodes, and the *New York Times* is angling to be sold for parts.

But that said: will the GOP stop playing Charlie Brown to the media's Lucy? If the Republican Party doesn't have the intestinal fortitude to fight back, it will be the growing numbers of disenchanted and disenfranchised Tea Party participants who will have to step up. And I want to foment their right-eous anger. These people are *my* people. They re-cognize the civilizational battle under way here; they understand that the United States is *it*, the last outpost for freedom. Ask any immigrant who strove to come here. They'll tell you.

I embraced the Tea Party movement because of its evocative use of a founding revolutionary re-bellion and its Constitution-mindedness. That was brought home even more deeply less than a year into the movement, when former Polish president and communist fighter Lech Walesa came to Illinois to support a Tea Party candidate. Why? "The United States was always the last resort and hope for all other nations," he said. "There was the hope that whenever there was something going wrong in the world, you could count on the United States. Today we've lost that hope." Walesa and others like him—people who have felt the oppression and the totalitarianism of the state at a fundamental level—understand that America is the beacon of freedom and liberty. That understanding is my lifeblood, the thing that motivates me and that motivates the Tea Party. I don't have a hard time saying that these notions of social justice and economic equality that sound so lovely to the left are the enemies of freedom and liberty. The Tea Party says it, too—and that's why the Complex wants to destroy it.

We have now entered the first full-fledged Alinsky presidency. And the only way to beat Alinsky is with strength. We don't fight fair; we fight righteous. The Democrats and President Obama will not give up their tack or their tactics. Do you think the GOP will win if its strategy is to apologize for every media-manufactured "right wing" outrage? It will not. We will win the day by using all the tools in our arsenal to fight the tyranny of these totalitarian ideologies that have been visited upon us from overseas, where those same ideologies caused only chronic human misery. We will win by using the New Media to expose the bankruptcy of their beliefs and tactics. And ultimately we'll win, because their ideas simply don't work. No amount of media spin can change that.

CHAPTER 10

The Big Plan: Join Us

Now you know the Complex, and you know that we can fight it if we just use the right tactics, understand our opponents, and walk toward the fire. *Walk toward the fire.* Don't worry about being called a racist, a homophobe, a sociopath, a violent heteronormative xenophobe with fascistic impulses. They say all those things about you because they're keeping you inside the Complex, forcing you to respond to their playbook. They want to stop you in your tracks. But if you keep going, if you tell them you can stop their verbal bullets and keep walking, you'll send messages to people who are rooting for you, who agree with you. That's how you build an invincible movement willing to play by its own rules.

Here's how I'm going to get you in that game.
Here's my plan.

* * *

I spent years working as a team player. But at a certain point, after watching other people take the risks and have successes and have failures, it became a personal imperative that I start sticking my neck out and emerging on my own. So after I left the Huffington Post and returned to Earth, I was determined to use my knowledge of the news cycle to create a brand—a media entity that could operate on a par with other news outlets, but that would use the New Media to even greater advantage. Breitbart.com and Breitbart.tv did that. People inside and outside the news business know the Breitbart sites: they've heard of them; they use and return to them. They learned fast that we had the newswires, and that we had the unique audio and video content.

It wasn't enough for me. *This isn't it*, I told myself. *This isn't going to define me—that I created a news aggregator, a generic media portal.*

The stage was set for the true Frankenstein monster to be unleashed.

My ultimate goal became to take the news aggregation-plus-group-blog model, build it up, and then implement my decade of New Media experience to make it explode into a genuine alternative news source. To turn the New Media into the media.

And I knew how to do it. I knew the flaw with sites like the Huffington Post that my own sites could avoid. HuffPo's structural weakness was that it was built upon people who were writing on any subject under the sun, often repetitiously. Mostly, that constituted, "Bush bad, Bush Hitler, Iraq War bad, blah blah blah." Under the amorphous banner of the Huffington Post, people wrote about whatever they wanted. Sure it sounds egalitarian and democratic and all that—but mostly it's just boring. There were even kids of Arianna's friends writing about the Dodgers. It hit me early on that the site lacked focus, that it was self-indulgent and repeated the media narrative.

And personally, I didn't want to end up like Arianna Huffington herself—a powerful but reactive person who went wherever the news cycle went, the person who would be able to answer any policy question because I'd studied the Hotline in the morning and the *Hill* in the evening, and stuck doggedly to that day's Democratic talking points. In fact, I didn't want to react to the news at all. I wanted to drive the news cycle.

So how is that different from what's gone before? Allow me an analogy.

My overarching analysis of the political gridiron is that mostly (not always), the Democrats are on the offense and the Republicans play a prevent defense. Sometimes Republicans win, but usually because Rush Limbaugh or some other defensive stud picks up a fumble or intercepts a pass at the two-yard line and runs it back ninety-eight yards for a touchdown. And the only reason defense has the chance to win at all on this playing field is because we are a center-right nation.

But we can no longer afford to hope defense wins us a ball game or two.

The Democrats have the Big Three Networks and major news dailies as their offensive line, and a starting backfield of Hollywood celebrities and academia.

Fortunately, however, the New Media comes with rules that level the playing field. The virtual newsroom at my Big websites, which you'll read about shortly, is an exercise in no-huddle offense, where citizen journalists can call audibles and get in the game. And it has forced the Democrat-Media Complex to finally play some defense. They've been caught off guard, and in the case of ACORN and elsewhere, the underdogs were able to upset the reigning Super Bowl champs.

What we need is more heady quarterbacks and risk-taking coaches to take on the powerhouses of the left. We need the revealing stories, the gutsy whistle-blowers, the unfiltered-by-the-Complex journalism. We need you. There is no reason not to play smashmouth ball, day in and day out, on both the political and the cultural fronts. Because, don't fool yourselves, that's exactly what they do.

It's the only way to break down the sclerotic news cycle they control—to get as many of us in the game as possible. On our side, to date, it's self-funded. While the Huffington Post has tens of millions of dollars to hire the best journalists in the world and to house itself in beautiful offices, we started the Bigs out of my basement for pennies. The right still has massive systemic handicaps in its media battles with the left. I've dedicated my entire business model—my entire life, really—to creating a way to combat those systemic deficiencies.

Over the next few years, the Bigs will expand beyond Hollywood (television, film, music), Journalism (media criticism), Government, and Peace (national security). We will take on Education, Tolerance (political correctness), and expand into Jerusalem (Middle East), EU (Old and New Europe), and beyond. The Big picture goes beyond America because the world is also under attack by the same anti–free market, anti–individual liberty forces. It is not just a political war, it is a cultural war, and our audacious goal is to change the big narrative.

Please, tell me it cannot be done!

Yes, we're targeting the left. But we're targeting

the right, too—and they know it. With the launch of each new Big site, the conservative establishment is learning that this model works, that there's stature to be gained from associating with the Bigs. Conservative intellectuals are seeing that it's worth being plugged into the New Media, that they can either sit in an office at a think tank and write white papers that may be read by a few hundred people and shape policy slightly, or they can drop bombs from a much higher elevation with much larger impact. And they can use the same skill set to do it. Sure, we need the maverick citizen journalists—the James O'Keefes and Patrick Courrielches and the tech-savvy kids—but we also need the Old Guard in the business suits to get out here on the front lines with us.

And you can be a part of it. Grab your digital recorder. Grab your BlackBerry or your iPhone. It's time to join the fight.

Because the Complex is in Big trouble.

Looking Ahead

In early October 2010, I flew to Houston to speak at a Tea Party. This one took place at a well-to-do planned community called the Woodlands. While there were about five thousand people in attendance—there was no media coverage. If the media couldn't say something mean about the Tea Party, they wouldn't say anything at all about it. But by this time, the Tea Party had successfully defended the attacks by the media and the Democratic Party, and it would become the machine that would radically alter the American political landscape on Election Day 2010.

What had started exclusively as an anti-intrusive, limited-government, political movement had naturally evolved into something more all-encompassing and cultural. With Tea Partiers stealing from the left-wing playbook (though it's tragic that it took us so long to figure out it was all Alinsky), conservatives had begun to learn the value of showing up, being vocal, and acting local. The American bourgeoisie was finally having its 1960s counterrevolution—and with a month left before the midterm election, people were starting to have fun.

I gave my maiden speech to the Tea Party on the off-off-main-stage event at the nationwide Tax Day 2009 Tea Partypalooza in Orange County, California, which is forty traffic-laden miles from my home. Not getting the choice Santa Monica Pier Tea Party gig—a mere five traffic-free miles from my home—turned out to be a blessing. Getting away from my comfort zone (and my zip code) set me on a course to see firsthand how the American spirit was still alive.

In Santa Ana, as I previously mentioned, I witnessed Ian Mitchell passionately wail his top hit, "Saturday Night," and also sing America's best patriotic songs with the passion of a newly minted citizen. From the beginning, the Tea Party was certainly not anti-immigrant! (In fact, at many subsequent Southern California Tea Parties, I would often run into some of my biggest fans—the Orozco family, who have a family coffee bean and espresso company and have indulged me with some of their finest beans!) My father-in-law, the formerly blacklisted actor Orson Bean, and another Big Hollywood contributor, thespian Gary Graham (*Alien Nation, Star Trek: Enterprise*), joined me onstage that day. The burgeoning conservative Hollywood movement, whose passion led to the creation of Big Hollywood, was taking its first baby steps out of the closet. I can tell you that the Tea Party has served as an inspiration to many in Hollywood who long for a saner American political future. Soon, I pray, America will see these patriots come out of the closet when the Complex implodes.

My antimainstream-media rants probably were not what the Republican National Committee would have ordered, but these off-the-cuff, pointed, stream-of-consciousness speeches resonated with Tea Party crowds state to state. (If I don't say so myself!) I used to worry a lot about speaking publicly. But speaking to Tea Parties was like speaking to friends and family, and I rarely left an event without new friends and culture warriors.

Tea Partiers, already steeped in the biased nature of American journalism, began to see their local and national media as clear impediments to achieving their political goals. And since I was screaming this tune, nearly savantlike, I was asked to be a keynote speaker at the first ever Tea Party Convention in Nashville, Tennessee, where I also had the privilege of introducing Sarah Palin.

Meeting her for the first time backstage, I told her how much I admired her refusal to cave in the face of repeated attempts by the media to assassinate her character, and that by her refusing to accept that they were shooting real bullets, she was teaching fellow patriots, and many gun-shy Hollywood conservative friends, that they could withstand similar predictable attacks. Regardless of what Palin represents to the political future of the Republican Party and the conservative movement, her cultural impact has been extraordinary.

It was such an honor to speak at so many Tea Party events. But it was perhaps the Houston Tea Party, a year and a half into it all, that made me finally realize that I was more than simply a defender of the Tea Party—I was truly a believer. These were my people. I walked through the crowd and I spoke to many of the speakers, to a group of veterans congregated together and enthusiastically cheering, to housewives, to African-Americans, to Hispanics—all sorts of people, all of whom had the same sense that the American people had finally awakened.

For the longest time, the left used activism and media to create the perception that they were a larger subsection of the American experience than they actually are. It was a smoke-and-mirrors game that the right allowed to stand unchallenged for way too long. By standing up for the Tea Party, by refusing to back down, by becoming one with them, I made it my mission to show the country that the Tea Party was a worthy grassroots conservative movement, and that the left was a corrupt political amalgam dominated by astroturfing organizations dedicated to the destruction of the country as we know it.

That mission made me a target.

The organized left, my stated enemy, saw me as a threat that needed to be destroyed — not just because I helped to take ACORN down, but because I started to recognize that we now had the tools to expose the left for what it is: a tightly connected group of unions and special-interest groups backed by George Soros and PR flacks paid for by Soros, like Media Matters and Organizing for America, and motivated media allies like the Huffington Post (quite a Frankenstein I created there, eh?) and, well, the entire mainstream media generally. In order to take down the organized left, I needed to shine a light on the organized left. And that was exactly what we did consistently throughout 2009 and 2010.

Which was one of the reasons why the Tea Party won.

The election of 2010 and, to a lesser degree, the off-year elections of 2009 acted as a confirmation that our message was getting through and that it wasn't just me alone, and the Big bloggers alone, that started to get the message and disseminate it. New and Social Media were the tools that the Tea Party would use to fight back and circumvent its well-funded "mainstream media" detractors.

The handheld video camera became the star of the New Media and the biggest weapon against the once-protected left's tactics of intimidation. Even though the networks mostly ignored the video footage that we collected—footage of the soon-to-be defeated congressman Bob Etheridge (D-NC) attacking a citizen; footage of an Organizing for America member and Democratic Party official calling me gay at an Organizing for America–sponsored "Stop the Hate Rally"; footage of ralliers at a Democratic Congressional Campaign Committee/Organizing for America/former Pelosi staffer–created event portraying Sarah Palin, Glenn Beck, and Adam Kinzinger as Nazis—we took the moral high ground and took away the left's tactics that had for so long been indulged and protected by the mainstream media. Our success forced a wedge between the mainstream media and the organized left, making it so they could no longer, without consequence, protect the Progressive political alliance.

In less than two years I felt more allied to the Tea Party than to the GOP. That sentiment is clearly shared by millions, and it now serves as a warning to the Republican establishment that the people are back in charge and on high alert.

Lessons from the Election

I knew a few key things going into the 2010 congressional midterms.

I knew that the Tea Party wasn't just a political movement—it had become an existential and a cultural movement. It had moved beyond politics and into the realm of everyday life for Americans who weren't separating their political viewpoints from their viewpoints on life anymore. Freedom wasn't just freedom to vote—it was freedom to live, and that need for freedom crossed all cultural, racial, and political boundaries.

After doing so many Tea Parties, it became obvious that strong-willed and educated women were leading the charge. In very few cases did I see men running things. This narrative—virtually untold by the media—is nevertheless self-evident when one sees how Sarah Palin and Rep. Michele Bachmann are tops in Tea Party popularity. It's the "mama grizzly" factor. And the more award-winning, feminist-neutral, objective, supermedia woman Katie Couric sneers at them, the more powerful they become.

While the media expended billions of dollars trying to label the Tea Party as racist, Lt. Col. Allen West and Tim Scott made history as Tea Party–endorsed congressional victors, both from the South. Perhaps their leadership skills and public stature will undo the negative branding of conservatives as racists. As I stated to the Uni-Tea rally in Philadelphia, this country and its Founders' ideals will not survive until *all* culturally Marxist subgroupings (race, gender, sexual orientation) embrace *E Pluribus Unum* — "one from many."

Significantly, when the impact of the Tea Party on the election was discussed on election night and thereafter, the "racism" meme had all but vanished. The fight against the N-word lie was dirty and ugly, but in the end we won and protected the reputation of the Tea Party. A huge victory.

I also understood, despite the media's getting it predictably oh-so-wrong, that the Tea Party wasn't merely a tool of the Republican Party. Many of the people I knew in the Republican Party — people who were longtime allies — reacted with fear and defensiveness with the rise of the movement that would, ironically, grant conservatism relevance and put it on offense where it always belonged. Many of those friends should heed the lessons of the 2010 midterms.

At its core, the Republican Party suffers from

whipped-dog syndrome. Its every word and policy is shaped by a defensiveness against its master—and its master is less Harry Reid and Nancy Pelosi than it is the mainstream media. Case in point: the last standard-bearer of the Republican Party was the defeated presidential candidate John McCain. McCain spent an entire political career cozying up to the media power structure in Washington, New York, and Hollywood. Then when he finally ran, expecting that he would be treated with dignity and respect for capitulating on core conservative principles, the media treated him like a mutt.

The Tea Party no longer wants to associate itself with this self-hating branch of the Republican Party. The GOP better know now not to trot out Senators Susan Collins and Olympia Snowe to placate their media masters.

Second, I knew that November 2 was a less important day for the movement than November 3 was.

The question was whether this once-in-a-lifetime awakening of conservatism would sustain itself. It's an open question. That's why I'm committed over the next two years to doing everything to keep that movement alive and trying to focus it on the right targets.

And the most important target? You guessed it: the mainstream media.

And it is going down, slowly but most surely. Its decline is evidenced by George Soros's last-minute, preelection cash infusion into NPR ($1.8 million) and Media Matters ($1 million). The MSM is so weak that its existing infrastructure needs to be buffered by a destructive, anti-American individual in order to ensure that even more ground isn't lost. To his credit, Soros understands that controlling the narrative is key, and media do that much better than the politicians—especially in the twenty-first century, a hypermedia age.

If the Tea Party made life miserable for individual congressmen simply by asking them basic questions like "Will you read the bill?" or "Do you support Obama's agenda?" and causing so much dismay and turmoil and consternation, what results can be wrought if the Tea Party brings its energy and tactics to bear on the media, which are even more vulnerable and corrupt and hypocritical than the Democratic Party they serve?

The year 2011 is the perfect time for the Tea Party to begin focusing on both local and national media and show that they can act as a check and balance against the media's natural tilt to the left. The Tea Party can show the mainstream media that if they don't clean up their act, they'll go the same way as the House Democrats in 2010. If you thought Democratic politicians were ham-fisted in responding to their constituents' concerns, imagine blow-dried reporters and Ivy League newsroom know-it-alls exposed to the YouTube light of day.

My third thought going into the election was a personal one related to my place in the media and political order. I noticed that in many pieces by the "objective" mainstream media, I was described as "ultraconservative" or "überconservative." But I bet these people can't even tell you what my position is on most political issues. Were they intentionally marginalizing me by calling me über- and ultraconservative without any clue that I voted for Proposition 19, which was an attempt to legalize marijuana in California? Were they labeling me in order to discredit me without even finding out that my agnostic sensibilities cause me to waver on the tectonic issue of gay marriage?

And then I realized that it didn't matter how they labeled me. At the end of the day, I know I'm not an aspiring political pundit, that I don't consider my voice any greater than my neighbor's voice, that my opinion on gay marriage is no more important than that of someone who is gay and is in a committed relationship, and that my thoughts on marijuana legalization are no more important than those of an orthodox Jew who has a deep problem with illegal drugs. I understood that if anybody thinks that my mission is to become another person you see on TV or hear on radio pontificating "It's my way or the highway" on such matters, they've completely missed my point.

I intentionally co-created the Huffington Post in order to grant the hard left a place in the blogosphere to express itself. I knew that in the future I wanted to provide a similar platform for citizen journalists who relate more to my way of thinking on the center right, on the side of individual freedoms and individual liberties and individual rights over group rights, group thinking, and categorizing people into racial, gender, and sexual-orientation categories only to then pit them against one another.

I co-created the Huffington Post and the Big sites as part of a grander strategy to knock down the false edifice that is the mainstream media, that is built upon the false proposition of "objective" journalism and the grotesque anti-American proposition of political correctness. My mission isn't to quash debate—it's to show that the mainstream media aren't mainstream, that their feigned objectivity isn't objective, and that open, rigorous debate is a positive good in our society.

Man, how I long for the days of Sam Kinison, Richard Pryor, Abbie Hoffman, Dr. Hunter S. Thompson, George Carlin, and Lenny Bruce. Today, the only people upholding their free-speech legacies are conservatives like Ann Coulter and Rush Limbaugh. And it's weird that most liberals, who seek to ban them from media appearances and NFL-team ownership, can't see that.

It's that mission to have a rigorous, no-holds-barred debate that made me a central part of this election cycle. Whether people read the Huffington Post on the left or my Big sites on the right, everyone is now disillusioned about the media. Nobody is fooled into believing that most reporters are objective, straight-down-the-middle truth-seekers. That means there's a greater transparency in the media. It doesn't mean that it's a calmer media—it doesn't mean that there isn't a lot of tumult and chaos out there—but I don't think our Founding Fathers would have considered a political-Prozac-addicted electorate to be the ideal.

I find it ironic that the same mainstream media that in 1992 lamented that my Generation X was not sufficiently engaged in politics are now upset that we are and have created New Media and Social Media, transforming them into a highly aggressive, deeply democratic, and rough-and-tumble environment that is now putting those former critics and overlords in the mainstream media into the unemployment line.

Election Night Revelation

When I was asked by ABC News to appear as a participant in its election night coverage, I at first considered the invitation a tacit acknowledgment that even a bastion of the mainstream media had heeded our message. With Big Journalism editor Dana Loesch in ABC's New York studio with George Stephanopoulos and Diane Sawyer, and me set to appear via satellite from the Walter Cronkite School of Journalism in Arizona before an audience of students, I thought, *Hmmm, maybe there is some progress.* The invitation had been in many ways righteously ironic. My primary critics had to recognize that the Tea Party they had denigrated consistently for two years had paved the way for massive political change, and the Tea Party's primary journalistic defender and the publisher of some of the biggest stories of that election cycle had to realize the benefit of asking me to be part of their election night coverage.

So, perhaps naïvely, I accepted the invitation and considered it to be a done deal.

It wasn't.

After accepting the invitation from ABC News, we posted an innocuous article at Big Journalism promoting the ABC News coverage that would feature Dana and me. In essence, we were simply asking our millions of readers to watch ABC. Some would call that free advertising.

Within hours, the organized left went after me (and ABC) with a meat cleaver. I found myself under the same level of organized attack that I had faced when the Shirley Sherrod incident occurred. (Speaking of which, you may have noticed that I don't discuss the Sherrod incident in this book. You probably know that Sherrod has threatened in the media to sue me. I can say this: there's a hell of a lot more to the Sherrod story than you've heard to this point. Stay tuned.)

Both the organized left's reaction to the Sherrod incident and their reaction to the ABC News story were retribution for my role in taking down ACORN and other sacred cows of the left. I had warned James O'Keefe and Hannah Giles that we would forever be marked targets. But knowing you're going to be hit doesn't take away from the sensation of being clobbered with a sucker punch.

Less than two days after the invitation, and less than twelve hours after the post announcing my participation in the broadcast, the organized left, led by my pals at Media Matters, ColorofChange.org (Van Jones!), CREDO (a Progressive phone company that sends a portion of one's bill to left-wing causes), Daily Kos, Talking Points

Memo, and my beautiful red-headed Frankenstein, the Huffington Post, assaulted ABC with at least 125,000 signatures and over 2,000 phone calls. By the time I woke up the next morning (a Saturday), there was already a hit piece in the *Washington Post* with an inside, unnamed source at ABC claiming that there was outrage inside the network's newsroom over the producer's picking me in the first place. "This blindsided a good portion of the team here," the source reportedly told Greg Sargent of the *Post*. "And not in a good way."[1]

The second insult-to-injury capitulation to the organized left was a concurrent statement by ABC News's David Ford, a PR flack, to Media Matters. Ford stated, "[Breitbart] will be one of many voices on our air, including Bill Adair of Politifact. If Andrew Breitbart says something that is incorrect, we have other voices to call him on it."[2] Upon reading it, I thought, *How naïve that I accepted this invitation. How naïve that I thought that ABC News would stand by its invitation and that the producer responsible for that invitation would act like a man and defend his pick.*

It got worse. Andrew Morse, the producer of the event for ABC, without even reaching out to me, issued a statement from ABC News that was described by the UK *Guardian* in accurate terms: "Breitbart claims he'll be appearing as an analyst, but a statement from ABC distances the network from him with comical vigour." Morse's statement explained that I was "not an ABC News consultant…not, in any way, affiliated with ABC News…not being paid by ABC News. He has not been asked to analyze the results of the election for ABC News. Mr. Breitbart will not be a part of the ABC News broadcast coverage…. He has been invited as one of several guests."[3]

Never mind that I never said anything to the contrary. But obviously, Morse had his job to preserve.

It was a line-by-line distancing and diminishing of my role in the event as a means to placate the left's desire for blood. I saw that my fate was sealed by looking to, of all people, former Clinton hit-job artist turned "objective" anchor, George Stephanopoulos, who tweeted, "Breitbart NOT on ABC network broadcast."

Ironically, my first memory of Stephanopoulos in conjunction with ABC News was in June 1996, when, while working in the Clinton White House, he threatened punitive action against the network that would later employ him to unbook as a guest a former FBI agent named Gary Aldrich, who reported wrongdoing at the Clinton White House. It still boggles the mind that Clinton's media hatchet man was soon thereafter rewarded with an anchor job and the mainstream media seal of objectivity.

But the saga wasn't done yet. I knew the ABC News brass had calculated that if they threw me under the bus completely, they risked the political right and Tea Party attacking ABC News for capitulating to the totalitarian left. So ABC News created an artificial wall—a digital Elba, if you will—where I would be exiled. They now said I would be participating only in an online forum—and, most egregiously, they lied that that had been the understanding from the very beginning. Jeffrey Schneider, a high-level ABC News PR flak, issued this statement: "Mr. Breitbart exaggerated the role he would play on his blog.... We immediately made it clear that was never the role he was supposed to play. He had been invited to be part of our digital town hall, and that is still the role."[4]

Every one of these acts by ABC News came in reaction to the left's push to get me kicked off the air. Every one of these acts was unilateral, without anybody from ABC News contacting me. They were throwing their invitee under the bus and they were doing so in a most cruel fashion. What was worse, they were calling me out as a liar. They were giving the anti–free speech forces of the left everything they wanted.

So I called Andrew Morse, whose entire attitude was narcissistic in the extreme. He simply couldn't believe that *he* was under such an assault by the organized left. I sympathized with him—for a while. Then I said, "Don't you understand how you're being used right now by the organized left? Don't you understand how they want me to lash back at ABC News so that it will confirm for them that I was a wrong and hostile choice in the first place?" I told him that I am very methodical in how I interrelate with the mainstream media, that I utilize a carrots-and-sticks approach: when you lie and you destroy, I fight back hard, but when you make the right moves, I reciprocate in kind.

I told Morse that I wanted to give ABC every opportunity to walk back their provably false allegation that I exaggerated my role. In fact, I held off responding publicly for well over a day in order to give them time to do so.

Meanwhile, ABC reiterated they wanted me in Phoenix.

"Oh, I'll be in Phoenix all right," I said, "because the ball is now in your court. All I have done is accepted your invitation and told my readers to watch ABC News on election night. Since then you've done everything wrong including lying, which confirms everything that my readers perceive about network news and the mainstream media.

"But," I continued, "I *am* going to put up the e-mail that you sent me, which confirms the invitation and clearly states that I am telling the truth and ABC News is lying." ABC News's answer by way of Morse: "Do what you have to do."

On Sunday night, I posted that e-mail. Here it is:

Andrew,

So great speaking with you, and I cannot thank you enough for joining us in Arizona on election night. We truly appreciate it.

NY is booking your travel right now, and want to make sure your name on your ID reads "Andrew Breitbart".

I really look forward to meeting you, and would love to take you out to lunch or dinner before our election coverage.

See below about ABC New's [*sic*] coverage on election night.

Cheers, and will see you soon.

XXXX

XXXX XXXX

Producer

ABC News

ABC News is conducting a live event from Phoenix, Arizona for our election night special on Tuesday, November 2nd 2010. I am looking for political figures and newsmakers to appear in our Town Hall style panel.

ABC News is providing live coverage of the

midterm elections hosted by Diane Sawyer and George Stephanopoulos in New York, and correspondents across the country.

ABC News has partnered with Facebook and The Cronkite School of Journalism at Arizona State University to live stream the entire event on abcnews.com, ABC News Now and Facebook.

The Town Hall is hosted by ABC correspondent David Muir and Randi Zuckerberg from Facebook, as well an ASU student leader.

The audience will consist of 150 students equipped with laptops and Ipads [*sic*] who will participate in online political conversations.

The issues include health care, the economy, immigration, terrorism, and the environment. We will have panelists who will contribute to these conversations remotely from Washington, DC, New York, NY and Los Angeles, CA.

This program will broadcast on the ABC Television Network, abcnews.com, ABC News Now, and ABC News Radio. The show will be live on the web and ABC News Now as well as on the network from 4:00 pm till 11:00 pm MST.

We would love for you to be a part of our program, and please let us know what we can do to accommodate your needs.

I am booking the guests for the event and will be in Phoenix starting Thursday, October 28th.

Feel free to email me back or call me at the following number with any questions.

Thanks so much,

XXXX XXXX

Producer

ABC News

After releasing the e-mail, on Monday, Jeffrey Schneider reiterated to my business partner that ABC wanted me to come to Phoenix. I spoke again with the producers at ABC News, who also told me they wanted to meet Monday night for dinner in Phoenix. Accordingly, I flew to Phoenix on Monday night to be part of ABC's election night coverage—in whatever capacity they should so choose. I knew they wanted me to drop out, but I was not going to give them the easy way out.

At about the time the producers were supposed to meet me for dinner on Monday night, I received a text from Morse saying that he was too busy preparing for the election coverage to attend dinner, and that they would be in touch early the next day.

The next morning, I called and texted almost continuously, asking where I should be, how I should dress, what topics would be discussed. No response...for four and a half hours. At around

12:30 p.m. (3:30 p.m. on the East Coast), just as I was supposed to leave for the event—at this point all news coverage around the country, including my own website, was all election results all the time—Morse sent me an e-mail disinviting me.

To add insult to injury yet again after picking at a scab that had been dashed with salt, ABC simultaneously sent the disinvitation to the left-wing media sites that had demanded I not participate on election night. They would revel in their victory as I packed to go back to LA, where at least now I could vote. To make matters worse, I was away from my office desk where I would be of best use on election night. ABC broke the news when those who would care were least interested in blowing up a minor media scandal and when the left needed a victory—any victory it could get, on what they knew was going to be a disaster of an election night for them. I was the left's Pyrrhic victory on Election Night 2010. I had been played.

But it was worth it! It was fun. Being the media is fun. Telling the truth is fun. Having an effect on the election cycle is fun. Getting into world-class battles with brand-name media players is fun. When you have the truth on your side and the American people behind you, it's fun! In hindsight, I wouldn't change a thing. In two short years we were not just building successful, impactful websites, but changing the way Americans read, consume, and create media. Fun, fun, fun!

What's Next?

I've already written that Election 2010 was less about November 2 than it was about November 3 and beyond.

For me, 2011 is going to be a recommitment toward a righteous attempt to level the playing field in the media; 2011 is going to be less about holding Nancy Pelosi and Harry Reid accountable than it's going to be about holding George Stephanopoulos, Andrew Morse, ABC News, and the rest of the mainstream media accountable. It's going to be about holding accountable the president of NPR, who capitulated to the exact same forces who attacked me when she canned Juan Williams and attacked his character in the process. It's going to be about holding George Soros and his Hungarian nut squat squad at Media Matters accountable. It's going to be about holding Arianna Huffington and Christiane Amanpour and Contessa Brewer and Katie Couric and Pinch Sulzberger accountable.

I am optimistic that the Tea Party movement is reflective of a greater American sentiment that needs to try at least to save what is good and decent about the American experience. Again, it is a cultural battle. And while they cling to their media guns and their politically correct religion, truth will be our weapon.

It's a long war. I know. I've lost friends. I have the scars. My wife married an almost inappropriately always-lighthearted guy fourteen years ago. Now she wakes up next to a firebrand who is one of the most polarizing figures in the country.

But I have also met the America that was rendered silent by the media and is now shaking itself to life again. These are the years that we will look back on and question whether we did enough for our country and for our children. That's why I'm so determined, so pissed, so righteously indignant.

Excuse me while I save the world.

Acknowledgments

First and foremost, I want to thank my wife, Susie. Long before I even met her, I was told by a friend, who has since passed away, that he met my future wife, a young, beautiful, and hysterically funny woman who at the time lived two thousand miles away. I am eternally grateful that Mike Gaybrant's fantastical prophecy came true.

To our amazing(ly large) family, Samson, Mia, Charlie, and Will: Too many people fought to create this country to squander it in a generation of greed and irresponsibility. I cannot stand on the sidelines as you and your generation are being handed the tab. You are beautiful, smart, and unconditionally loved, and I hope that I inspire you to become strong individualists—even if that means sometimes disagreeing with your headstrong father.

To Larry Solov: At first a friend, and second, my most trusted adviser. You have made so many quiet sacrifices to join this business turned cultural, political, and media war. I admire you for your intense loyalty, for looking after the things I don't always want to see, and for balancing your two worlds to make things work for us. I hope one day you can look back and realize how much of this fight is inspired by you and your moral compass and decency. Thanks for not having ADHD, too. That would really, really suck. Our friendship is cherished more than words can describe.

To my mother, Arlene, and my sister, Tracey, and her beautiful family (husband Brian, and children Ben, Jake, and Lola): Thanks for your constant support and love. Thanks, Mom, for instilling that distinct guilt complex that makes making the right and moral decision a necessity.

To Orson and Ally: Two of the more important role models in my life. Orson, you've taught me how to mix the magic formula of truth, conviction, humor, and point of view. Let's see how it works out! Ally, your compassion and decency are an inspiration. You have done more to make our extended family gel than anyone else. Your and Orson's prayers do not go unnoticed. Thanks for putting in a good word with the Big Guy.

To Carolyn, Mimi, Marc (the most talented man

I know), Max, Zeke, Rosemary, Calvin, Zelly, Georgia, et al.: The degree to which you agree or disagree with me politically doesn't change a thing about how grateful I am to have you as my family. That goes for Georgia, especially! Vote Chris Christie '12!

To the Big Editors: There's rarely a week that goes by that I don't think out of the blue about how "lucky" we got with our first editor pick, John Nolte. Yes, he is the conscience of "the Bigs" — but when the wars begin, he is the first to grab a weapon and fight the good fight. Michael Flynn, a longtime friend and trench warrior, was the right man at the right time to run Big Government and to make sense of the wild new Obama/Pelosi/Reid big-government terrain. After fighting the activist left for so many years, his collaboration in the group takedown of mighty, mighty corrupt ACORN is his place in history. First the erudite combatant Michael Walsh, and now the elegant warrior Dana Loesch, Big Journalism is a central part of the Bigs mission: it's not just the corrupt politicians who need to be held in check, but, as Sarah Palin called them, "the corrupt bastards" of the media who use the false veil of objectivity to fight so consistently and mercilessly against those who reject their rigid "Progressive" goals. Over at Big Peace we have our resident scholar, Peter

Schweizer. Sometimes the guilt gets to be too much thinking that we rushed this impeccable gentleman into Animal House. We're so glad his sobriety is there to tame our overenthusiasm from time to time. And we're even more grateful he stands with us when the going gets tough. Our latest editor, Larry O'Connor, entered the fray as a contributor and became a must-hire from day one and is family. And, last and most certainly not least, Alex Marlow. Alex was our first hire, and is arguably the most important person in the entire enterprise. With that admission, you are now a marked man. You have earned every ounce of my respect for you. In fifteen years when you need me to vouch for your character, you know I'll be there singing your many talents and virtues. Wink, wink.

To the Big Contributors: You are my business model. When we set out to design the twenty-first-century virtual newspaper, we knew it had to be powered by you, the citizen journalist: the doctor, the lawyer, and the schoolteacher ready and willing to break the stories the mainstream media conspicuously ignore, and join us in the fight to change politics and the media for the better. You're in the fight for the best of reasons: to preserve the future of this great nation. For the hours you've put in with nary a paycheck and rarely a thank-you to show for it, you've been ruffling all the right feathers and changing not only the discussion, but how it's discussed. You've redefined what a newsroom means in this day and age, and countless times, you've beaten the Old Media at their own game — and believe me, they don't like it. When we have a real newsroom with a real infrastructure, I cannot wait to spend my time calling each and every one of you to thank you for your heroic wares.

Drudge, thanks for *everything*.

Steve Bannon, thanks for becoming a front-and-center confidant and friend in no time flat. Your values, intelligence, generosity and guidance have been invaluable. Happy to be a grundoon in your service.

John Fund, thanks for your Obi-Wan Kenobi–like guidance through the political and news cycles. And of course I cherish our friendship deeply.

Ben Shapiro, a better sounding board I could not find. We're an odd pair. We are nearly mathematical opposites, but fighting the same fight for virtually the same reasons. Is that the commutative property? (Math was never my best subject.) You have no idea how glad I am I reached out to you when I saw you fighting the good fight as a seventeen-year-old sophomore at the UCLA *Daily Bruin*. Then I couldn't believe someone courageous like you existed. Nine years later, I feel the exact same.

Darren Rush, Adrian Otto, and Gerald Chao, you know too well my technical shortcomings as that Internet guy and make me look good nonetheless.

Dennis Miller, I am eternally grateful for you supporting me and my work from the very, very beginning. Apostasy wouldn't be half as fun without knowing THE Dennis Miller's seeing the same things, too. Also, for whatever reason, one of your lines has stuck in my head for over twenty years: "'Jimmy cracked corn, and I don't care.' What in the hell sort of attitude is that?" Kills me.

Rush Limbaugh, your astounding success is a beacon for every aspiring voice on the radio and every "blogger" on the Internet. Like Reagan, you led this revolution with good cheer and humor—kryptonite to the left. On a selfish note, becoming friends with one of my heroes has been a highlight of my life.

Sean Hannity, aside from your guidance, support, and friendship, you are also a role model for the way you balance your public and family life all the while maintaining your exemplary character.

Ann Coulter, though our body types are noticeably dissimilar, it is you who I've always aspired to be—the most courageous warrior in the movement. With precision and Vegas-headliner humor, you dismantle the left daily and stop their transparent antics in their tracks. You're a great mentor and a better friend.

Mark Masters, thanks for dropping out of school and selling puka shells. You are an immense inspiration, a general, and a good friend.

Laura Ingraham, when I was getting clobbered, you stood out, defending me when it was not the politically expedient thing to do. And boy, did I notice.

Mark Levin, your book *Liberty and Tyranny* is the most important book of recent memory. Its timely release as the Tea Party grew and thrived was divine. History is going to look fondly on you, and I will be happy to say that a ferocious and defiant patriot was a friend.

Hugh Hewitt, you're the first place I know I can go to unravel the most complex issues of our time, sometimes even when they involve me. Thanks for sticking up for me even when others didn't.

Patrick Courrielche, thanks for showing exemplary courage—and for understanding that art and culture are more influential than politics.

James O'Keefe and Hannah Giles, you earned your place in media history. Sorry Jann Wenner never saw fit to put you on the cover of *Rolling Stone*. His loss. Your futures are bright.

Greg Gutfeld, you've done more to alter the image of conservatives for America's Utes than any other 3 a.m. late-night cable news talk show host. In all seriousness, it's amazing that two guys so similarly unserious in our comparable upbringings have realized there's more to life than finding cool music before others. Thanks for all.

Glenn Beck, Bill O'Reilly, and Megyn Kelly, thanks for seeing the subtle, grotesque details that turned the ACORN exposé into a pivotal 3-D *Avatar*-like news-watching experience.

Rusty Humphries, Lars Larson, Greg Garrison, thanks for making me a regular part of your radio diet.

Michael Savage, my next book will be a controversial exposé that you are cuddly, warm, affectionate, hysterically funny, and easy to get along with.

Mike and Diane Silver, our luck in happening upon the two of you as neighbors is going down as one of life's greatest unexpected gifts. Thanks for looking after my wife and family when I am in outer space.

Adam Baldwin, a happy warrior and at times, literally, my bodyguard.

Gary Hewson, real estate development, my ass! You're an investigative journalist legend!

Paul Mauro, many thanks for your insights and assistance—and for what you do during the day.

In no particular order, and whose friendship and support, regardless of politics, I cherish: Maura

Flynn, Christian Josi, Andrew Marcus, Evan Maloney, Jude, Ken LeCorte, Tim Hale, John Ondrasik, Glenn Reynolds, Chip Gerdes, Christian Bladt, Jon Kahn, Liberty Chick, Dan Riehl, Flint Dille, David Greenfield, Patrick Frye, Frank Miller, Kimberly Cox, Scott Kaufer, Mike Sullivan, Scott Johnson, John Hinderaker, Patrick Dollard, Mickey Kaus, Scott Johnson, Kevin Reilly, Tucker Carlson, Judit Maull, Rob Long, Lee Stranahan, Evan Sayet, Steve Hayes, Allen Covert, Dr. Jeff Gandin, Rep. Michele Bachmann, Rep. Steve King, Rep. Thaddeus McCotter, Dan Basmagian, John Reimers, Matt Labash, John Irwin, Kathryn Lopez, D. B. Sweeney, Paul Raff, Gary Sinise, Brian Kennedy, The Claremont Institute, Charles Kesler, Tammy Haddad, Ben Robin, Joe Escalante, Robert Davi, Seth Swirsky, Bill Whittle, Jon Fleischman, Andrew Klavan, Jeremy Boreing, the Harrahs (Richard, Verna, and Julie), John L'Herault, Michael Nadlman, Katie O'Malley, Kurt Loder, Tammy Bruce, Jonah Goldberg, Bill Sammon, Charles Winecoff, Mike Roman, Christian Adams, Niger Innis, Brandon Darby, Ned Rice, Joel Pollack, Billy Zoom, John Podhoretz, Lucianne Goldberg, Victoria Jackson, Jon Voight, Brian Iglesias, Melanie Morgan, Debbi Lee, Frank Gaffney, David Reaboi, Matthew Marsden, Jason Jones, Tarina Tarantino, Alfonso Campos, Steve McEveety,

Jim Caviezel, Amy Holmes, Chad Fleming, and Jamie Hailer.

To those I forgot to mention by name: I sincerely apologize. And refuse to invoke ADHD yet again. Besides, it just means you'll for sure be mentioned in the next book.

To Gene Brissie and Rick Wolff, without whom this book would not exist: Thanks for believing in me and my story, and pretending to overlook my ADHD.

To the Tea Party patriots I have met over the last year: Thank you for getting off your butts, leading the revolution, and withstanding the unfounded, predictable media attacks. We made history.

Notes

CHAPTER 1: From Little ACORNs Grow...

1 Cristina Corbin, "ACORN to Play Role in 2010 Census," FoxNews.com, March 18, 2009, http://www.foxnews.com/politics/2009/03/18/acorn-play-role-census/.

CHAPTER 3: Thank God for the Internet

1 "Ants in the Picnic Basket?" DrudgeReport.com, July 4, 1997, http://www.drudgereportarchives.com/dsp/specialReports_pc_carden_detail.htm?reportID= {F996E731-A796-400C-9B0D-D91F3FAB6BBE}.
2 "White House First Learned Willey Was Talking during Online Chat," DrudgeReport.com, March 15, 1998, http://www.drudgereportarchives.com/dsp/specialReports_pc_carden_detail.htm?reportID= {EFC06A59-502F-4477-806C-954B06564D1A}.
3 Arianna Huffington, "Tomb of the Well-Known Hotel Magnate," AriannaOnline.com, November 24, 1997, http://ariannaonline.huffingtonpost.com/columns/column.php?id=597.
4 Maureen Dowd, "For Once, Clinton Was Innocent," *Wilmington Morning Star*, November 25, 1997.
5 Arianna Huffington, "The Ancient Non-Mariner," AriannaOnline.com, December 4, 1997, http://ariannaonline.huffingtonpost.com/columns/column.php?id=600.
6 Ibid.

7 "Newsweek Kills Story on White House Intern," Drudge Report.com, January 17, 1998, http://www.drudgereportarchives.com/data/2003/01/16/20030116_014732_ml.htm.

CHAPTER 4: Hey, Old Media: It's Not Your Business Model That Sucks, It's You That Suck

1 Kate Zernike, "CPAC Speaker Bashes Obama, in Racial Tones," *New York Times*, February 18, 2010, http://thecaucus.blogs.nytimes.com/2010/02/18/cpac-speaker-bashes-obama-in-racial-tones/.

2 Alicia C. Shepard, "A Scandal Unfolds," *American Journalism Review*, March 1998, http://www.ajr.org/article.asp?rel=ajrshepard1_mar98.html.

3 Marvin L. Kalb, *One Scandalous Story: Clinton, Lewinsky, and the Thirteen Days That Tarnished American Journalism* (New York: Free Press, 2001), 90–91.

4 Shepard, "A Scandal Unfolds."

5 Ibid.

6 Kalb, *One Scandalous Story*, 94–95.

7 Shepard, "A Scandal Unfolds."

8 "Report: Lewinsky Offered U.N. Job; Investigators: DNA Trail May Exist," DrudgeReport.com, January 21, 1998, http://www.drudgereportarchives.com/data/2002/01/17/20020117_175502_ml.htm.

9 *Today*, NBC, January 27, 1998.

10 "She Had Sex with Cigar: Media Struggles with Shocking New Details of White House Affair," DrudgeReport.com, August 22, 1998, http://www.drudgereportarchives.com/data/2003/01/16/20030116_014732_ml.htm.

11 "Storm over Lewinsky 'Stalker' Claim," BBC News, February 8, 1999, http://news.bbc.co.uk/2/hi/events/clinton_under_fire/latest_news/274792.stm.

12 Associated Press, "Lewinsky 'Stalker' Label Tied to Blumenthal," *Toledo Blade*, February 7, 1999.

13 Sidney Blumenthal, *The Clinton Wars* (Farrar, Straus and Giroux, 2003), 371.

14 Christopher Hitchens, "Thinking Like an Apparatchick," *Atlantic*, July–August 2003.

15 Gabriel García Márquez, "Why My Friend Bill Had to Lie," *Guardian* (UK), January 30, 1999.

16 Richard Goldstein, "Sexual McCarthyism: Lurid Revelations, Crude Moralizing, Perjury Traps: They All Echo America's Darkest Days," *Village Voice*, September 29, 1998.

17 Kathy Kiely, "The Prez Sleuth Terry Lenzner Made a Name Exposing Dirty Tricksters. But Now This Ex–New Yorker Is Accused of Being One," *New York Daily News*, March 8, 1998.

18 John M. Broder, "White House and Starr Clash on Subpoenas," *New York Times*, February 25, 1998.

19 Ann Coulter, "Between Consenting Adulteries: Bill Clinton's Bimbo M.O.," *Human Events*, February 6, 1998.

20 Jonathan Broder and Harry Jaffe, "Clinton's Sexual Scorched-Earth Plan," Salon.com, August 5, 1998, http://www.salon.com/news/1998/08/05news.html.

21 David Talbot, " 'This Hypocrite Broke Up My Family,' " Salon.com, September 16, 1998, http://www.salon.com/news/1998/09/cov_16newsb.html.

22 "Why We Ran the Henry Hyde Story," editorial, Salon.com, September 16, 1998, http://www.salon.com/news/1998/09/16newsc.html.

23 Larry Flynt, *Sex, Lies & Politics: The Naked Truth* (New York: Kensington Books, 2004), 13–14.

24 Ibid., 16.

25 David Neiwert, "Lives of the Republicans, Part Two," Salon.com, September 16, 1998, http://www.salon.com/news/1998/09/16news.html.

26 Jason Vest, "Secret Lives of the Republicans, Part One," Salon.com, September 11, 1998, http://www.salon.com/news/

1998/09/11newsb.html.

27 Darrell M. West, *The Rise and Fall of the Media Establishment* (New York: Palgrave Macmillan, 2001), 100.

28 Dan Savage, "Stalking Gary Bauer," Salon.com, January 25, 2000, http://dir.salon.com/politics2000/feature/2000/01/25/bauer/index.html.

29 "The Firestorm over 'Stalking Gary Bauer,'" editorial, Salon.com, January 29, 2000, http://dir.salon.com/politics2000/feature/2000/01/29/savage_reaction/index.html.

CHAPTER 5: The Democrat-Media Complex Strikes Back

1   Kevin Sack, "The 43rd President: After the Vote—A Special Report," *New York Times*, December 15, 2000.

2   Richard S. Dunham, "Who Says Bush Has a Mandate? Bush," BusinessWeek.com, February 20, 2001, http://www.businessweek.com/bwdaily/dnflash/feb2001/nf20010220_680.htm.

3   "What Mr. Bush Can Do," editorial, *New York Times*, December 15, 2000.

4   Ann Coulter, *Slander* (New York: Crown Publishers, 2002), 33–34.

5   Maureen Dowd, "Liberties; Mexico Likes Us!," *New York Times*, May 6, 2001.

6   Howard Fineman, "A President Finds His True Voice," *Newsweek*, September 24, 2001, http://www.newsweek.com/2001/09/23/a-president-finds-his-true-voice.html.

7   Richard L. Berke, "A Nation Challenged: The Democrats; Bush Winning Gore Backers' High Praises," *New York Times*, October 20, 2001.

8   Laura Ingraham, *Shut Up and Sing* (Washington: Regnery, 2003), 77–78.

9   Greg Pierce, *Washington Times*, January 23, 2003, available at http://goliath.ecnext.com/coms2/gi_0199-939012/Marching-or-

ders.html.

10 Ingraham, *Shut Up and Sing*, 77–83.

11 Bernard Zuel, "Lights, Camera, Take Action: Sarandon Rallies the Arts," *Sydney Morning Herald*, November 19, 2002.

12 Jay Stone, "Sundance Still Relevant," *Vancouver Sun*, January 21, 2003.

13 Tim Robbins, "A Chill Wind Is Blowing in This Nation...," CommonDreams.org, April 15, 2003, http://www.commondreams.org/views03/0416-01.htm.

14 Sean Penn, "An Open Letter to the President of the United States of America: Advertisement," *Washington Post*, October 18, 2002.

15 Dinesh D'Souza, *The Enemy At Home* (New York: Broadway Books, 2007), 50.

16 Andrew Sullivan, "Why Is This Race Even Close?" Salon.com, November 6, 2000, http://www.salon.com/news/politics/feature/2000/11/06/bush.

17 Andrew Sullivan, "Stand By Our Man," Salon.com, September 18, 2001, http://www.salon.com/news/politics/feature/2001/09/18/bush.

18 Andrew Sullivan, "War Is Declared," The Daily Dish, TheAtlantic.com, February 24, 2004, http://sullivanarchives.theatlantic.com/index.php.dish_inc-archives.2004_02_22_dish_archive.html.

19 Rob Reiner, "Where Have You Gone, Woodward & Bernstein?" HuffingtonPost.com, May 10, 2005, http://www.huffingtonpost.com/rob-reiner/where-have-you-gone-woodw_b_579.html.

CHAPTER 6: Breakthrough

1 Theodore Roosevelt, "Who Is a Progressive?" April 1912, available at http://teachingamericanhistory.org/library/index.asp?document=1199.

2 Theodore Roosevelt, "The New Nationalism," 1910, available at http://teachingamericanhistory.org/library/index.asp?document=501.

3 Quoted in Thomas E. Woods, *33 Questions About American History You're Not Supposed to Ask* (New York: Crown Forum, 2007), 138.

4 Ronald J. Pestritto, *Woodrow Wilson and the Roots of Modern Liberalism* (Lanham, MD: Rowman & Littlefield, 2005), 75.

5 Ronald J. Pestritto, *Woodrow Wilson: The Essential Political Writings* (Lanham, MD: Rowman & Littlefield, 2005), 78.

6 Christopher Lasch, *Haven in a Heartless World: The Family Besieged* (New York: W. W. Norton, 1995), 86.

7 As quoted in Chilton Williamson, *The Conservative Bookshelf* (Secaucus, NJ: Citadel Press, 2005), 296.

8 Max Horkheimer, *Critical Theory: Selected Essays* (New York: Continuum, 2002), 207.

9 Ibid., 218–19.

10 As quoted in Patrick Buchanan, *The Death of the West* (New York: Thomas Dunne Books, 2001), 86.

11 Adam Cohen, "What's Hot on This BBC Podcast? The Siege of Munster (1534–35)," *New York Times*, February 17, 2010.

12 Erich Fromm, *The Fear of Freedom* (London: Routledge, 1984), 241.

13 Ibid., 145–46.

14 Wilhelm Reich, *The Sexual Revolution: Toward a Self-Governing Character Structure* (New York: Macmillan, 1962), 77–78, 111, 184.

15 Thomas Maier, *Dr. Spock: An American Life* (New York: Basic Books, 2003), 112, 458.

16 Theodor Adorno, *The Culture Industry* (London: Routledge, 2003), 99.

17 Jonah Goldberg, *Liberal Fascism: The Secret History of the American Left, from Mussolini to the Politics of Change* (New York: Broadway Books, 2007), 175.

18 Herbert Marcuse, *Eros and Civilization: A Philosophical Inquiry*

into Freud (Boston: Beacon Press, 1966), 81, 226.

19 Herbert Marcuse, *An Essay on Liberation* (Boston: Beacon Press, 1969), 46–47.

20 Herbert Marcuse, "Repressive Tolerance," in Robert Paul Wolff, Barrington Moore Jr., and Herbert Marcuse, *A Critique of Pure Tolerance* (Boston: Beacon Press, 1969), 95–137.

21 Mao Zedong, "Where Do Correct Ideas Come From?" May 1963. Pamphlet, Foreign Languages Press, 1966, 3 pages.

22 Harry Chatten Boyte and Nancy N. Kari, *Building America: The Democratic Promise of Public Work* (Philadelphia: Temple University Press, 1996), 102.

23 "Essay: Radical Saul Alinsky: Prophet of Power to the People," *Time*, March 2, 1970.

24 Saul D. Alinsky, *Rules for Radicals: A Pragmatic Primer for Realistic Radicals* (New York: Vintage Books, 1989).

25 Ibid., xiii, xvi, xxi.

26 Ibid., xix.

27 Ibid., xxiv–xxv.

28 Ibid., 4.

29 Ibid., 21.

30 Ibid., 9–10.

31 Ibid., 6.

32 Ibid., 17.

33 Ibid., 33.

34 Ibid., 60.

35 Ibid., 136–138.

36 Ibid., 139.

CHAPTER 7: Pragmatic Primer for Realistic Revolutionaries

1 *Real Time with Bill Maher*, March 13, 2009, HBO.

2 Jack Cashill, "Who Wrote Dreams from My Father?" American Thinker, October 9, 2008, www.americanthinker.com/2008/10/who_wrote_dreams_from_my_fathe_1.html.

CHAPTER 8: The Abu Ghraib of the Great Society

1 Andrew Breitbart, "Couric Should Look in Mirror," *Washington Times*, September 7, 2009.
2 "ACORN Fires 2 Employees After Hidden Camera Stunt," WBALTV.com, September 10, 2009, http://www.wbaltv.com/ news/20841755/detail.html.
3 Jake Tapper, "Census Severs Relationship with ACORN," ABCNews.com, September 11, 2009, http://blogs.abcnews.com/politicalpunch/2009/09/census-severs-relationship-with-acorn.html.
4 "Congress Votes to Strip ACORN of Federal Funding," FoxNews.com, September 15, 2009, http://www.foxnews.com/ politics/2009/09/17/congress-votes-strip-acorn-federal-funding/.
5 "Issa Releases Investigative Report Finding ACORN Still Alive and Well," Republicans.oversight.house.gov, April 1, 2010.

CHAPTER 9: Tea Party Protector

1 "Fear or Loathing: Democrats Raise Specter of Swastikas to Cancel Town Meetings," FoxNews.com, August 6, 2009, http://www.foxnews.com/politics/2009/08/06/fear-loathing-democrats-raise-specter-swastikas-cancel-town-halls/.
2 Andrew Breitbart, "2010: A Race Odyssey—Disproving a Negative for Cash Prizes or, How the Civil Rights Movement Jumped the Shark," BigGovernment.com, March 25, 2010, http://biggovernment.com/abreitbart/2010/03/25/2010-a-race-odyssey-disproving-a-negative-for-cash-prizes-or-how-the-civil-rights-movement-jumped-the-shark/.

EPILOGUE: Looking Ahead

1 Greg Sargent, "Source: ABC's Newsroom Upset with Decision to Tap Andrew Breitbart," The Plum Line, WashingtonPost

.com, October 30, 2010, http://voices.washingtonpost.com/plum-line/2010/10/source_abcs_newsroom_upset_wit.html.

2 Matt Gertz, "Failing Upward: Breitbart to Be Featured in ABC's 2010 Election Coverage," MediaMatters.org, October 29, 2010, http://mediamatters.org/blog/201010290035.

3 Oliver Burkeman, "US Midterms Diary: John McCain's Penthouse Put-Down," *Guardian* (UK), November 1, 2010, http://www.guardian.co.uk/world/2010/nov/01/midterms-diary-mccain-reid-palin.

4 Michael Calderone, "Breitbart, ABC News Spar over His Election Night Role," The Upshot, Yahoo.com, November 1, 2010, http://news.yahoo.com/s/yblog_upshot/20101101/el_yblog_upshot/breitbart-abc-news-spar-over-election-night-role.

About the Author

Part publisher, part agent provocateur, part blogger, but all high-octane, politically incorrect truth-teller and mainstream media destroyer, Andrew Breitbart defies easy categorization.

Described as "überconservative" by his many political enemies, he co-created the Huffington Post. A free-speech advocate, he believes that there need to be more voices and more dissension in our democracy, not homogenized mainstream media pabulum. As a result, in 2009, he began to launch a series of groundbreaking group blogs harnessing a combustible mix of opinion, breaking news, and good old-fashioned investigative journalism, all aimed directly at the power structure of Hollywood, the mainstream media, and the political establishment. The Breitbart network presently includes Breitbart.com, Breitbart.tv, Big Government, Big Hollywood, Big Journalism, and Big Peace, with more to come in 2011.

With a fierce independence of spirit fueled by thousands of like-minded patriots and rebels, the "Bigs" took down ACORN and tapped into, defended, and propelled the Tea Party, leading the charge into the historic 2010 elections. As the Old Media falls apart, Breitbart leads a populist uprising to redefine media, politics, and culture.

Andrew Breitbart lives in Los Angeles with his wife, three sons, and a daughter.